STORIES OF

TRANSGRESSION

& Recovery

FROM THOSE AFFECTED BY ADDICTION & TRAUMA

COMPILED BY TRUNNIS GOGGINS II

Published By: DNP Presents

Library of Congress Cataloging-in-Publication Data has been applied for

ISBN: 979-8-9999454-4-0

PRINTED IN THE UNITED STATES OF AMERICA

Disclaimer

This book contains mature themes, including references to addiction, trauma, sexual situations, strong language, and graphic descriptions of real-life experiences. These stories are raw and authentic, written to shed light on the realities of struggle, survival, and recovery.

Reader discretion is advised.

The views, thoughts, and experiences shared in this book belong to the individual authors. This book is intended for educational, inspirational, and testimonial purposes only and should not be considered a substitute for professional counseling, medical advice, or treatment.

If you or someone you know is struggling with addiction, abuse, or mental health challenges, please seek support from a qualified professional or reach out to local crisis and recovery resources.

TABLE OF CONTENTS

Introduction: Trunnis Goggins II 7

The Story of Ryan Mader 21

The Story of Scott Free 47

The Story of Darcy Frederick........................... 62

The Story of Shalyn Patrick 85

The Story of Dr. Angela Bennett 104

The Story of Shonna Frye 127

The Story of Bronwen Healy 139

The Story of Gail Howell 161

A Story from One Affected by Addiction & Trama by
Dr. Sonya Howell Barrow 174

The Story of Erin Sparks 197

The Story of Tessa Williams 213

Resources and Helplines 304

Introduction Chapter

Trunnis Goggins, II

Addiction is an insidious force—one that transcends boundaries of class, color, culture, and creed. It does not discriminate based on wealth, heritage, political power, or social prestige. It quietly creeps into households, ruptures bonds, and dismantles dreams, often without warning. Its reach extends from the humblest homes to the highest halls of power, including the story of America's Founding Fathers.

One such story is that of John Adams, the second President of the United States. His son, Charles Adams, was a brilliant man who struggled with alcoholism for most of his adult life. In an emotionally gripping moment portrayed in an HBO special on John Adams, we see the heartbreak of a father confronting the reality of his son's addiction. Upon finding Charles drunk and disoriented, John tearfully utters, "I renounce you," before breaking down—a scene that embodies the helplessness and devastation many families experience.

Although dramatized, that moment is deeply rooted in reality. It mirrors countless conversations, confrontations, and collapses occurring every day across the world. Many of us recognize something of our own journeys in Charles Adams' story—the pain of watching a loved one spiral, and the emotional scars left behind. While John Adams' renunciation of his son may seem extreme, both for his time and ours, the tears he shed are timeless and universally understood.

Regarding Charles' wife, Sarah (also known as Sally), history offers conflicting accounts—some say she left him, others suggest he abandoned the family. Either way, Sally made the difficult yet necessary decision to return to Massachusetts and live with the Adams family. While it's often said that a spouse should stand by their addicted partner, there are times when destructive behavior endangers the entire household. In those cases, taking protective action may not only be wise—it may be lifesaving.

Sometimes such action can lead to healing and recovery for both parties. Other times, it may accelerate the addicted individual's decline. In my life, I've witnessed both outcomes. I've seen relationships salvaged by the courage to walk away, and I've seen heartbreaking loss when the addicted partner spiraled beyond return. Even years later, some families still carry the emotional toll of that descent.

As the fourth book in the Stories Of series, this volume is unique. It offers real-time hope. This is the first book in the series that not only tells powerful stories but also equips readers to take actionable steps toward healing and change. Within these pages, you will find a chorus of voices—survivors, healers, and thrivers—each offering a roadmap out of darkness.

Stories of Transgression and Recovery is not just a compilation of pain. It is a declaration of perseverance. It is a collection of lives reclaimed. And most importantly, it is proof that no matter how far one may fall, recovery and redemption are always within reach.

Addiction Does Not Respect Boundaries

Addiction does not respect boundaries. It appears in stories as old as the United States itself and remains a prominent issue today. Former First Lady Betty Ford is a powerful example. After confronting her own addiction to alcohol and prescription pills, she used her platform to help others, founding the Betty Ford Center—a sanctuary that continues to offer healing and hope to countless individuals.

I deeply admire the story of Betty Ford because she recognized the destruction caused by her addiction and made a conscious choice to give back. She leveraged her influence, notoriety, and connections to become a catalyst for recovery. Thousands of people are helped every day because she was willing to reach back and support those who were once where she had been.

In this book, you will see similar stories—individuals who have endured the darkness of addiction and emerged with a desire to help others. These survivors, regardless of the path they took to recovery, are nothing short of heroes. They use their experiences not as scars to hide, but as tools to uplift those still in the struggle.

Addiction is no stranger to the highest offices in the land. Consider Franklin Pierce, the 14th President of the United States, who was known to be a heavy drinker. His alcoholism worsened after the tragic deaths of his children, especially his youngest son Benjamin, who died in a train accident just before Pierce's inauguration. Some historians suggest that Pierce's alcoholism and emotional turmoil contributed to the indecision and lack of leadership that ultimately hastened the country's descent into civil war.

In more recent history, Richard Nixon, who preceded Gerald and Betty Ford in the White House, was also rumored to struggle with alcohol and prescription pill abuse. His condition allegedly became so severe that, in the final days of his presidency, the nuclear codes were withheld from him by military officials.

Addiction is equally rampant in the corporate world. As a child, I remember the fall of John DeLorean, the automotive innovator behind the iconic DeLorean car. Once a celebrated CEO, his legacy was marred by scandal and drug charges. Athletes, too, have frequently fallen victim to addiction—often at the cost of their careers. I think of Len Bias, the brilliant basketball prospect drafted by the Boston Celtics, who died of a cocaine overdose just days after being drafted. On the flip side, stories of recovery, such as that of Darryl Strawberry, give hope that redemption is possible.

I, too, have witnessed addiction destroy lives close to me. My brother's memoir, *Can't Hurt Me*, details the chaos our father brought into our home—chaos fueled by bottles of J&B Scotch, Dewar's White Label, and Chivas Regal. When the alcohol ended, prescription painkillers took their place. My father, despite being a gifted businessman, allowed addiction to unravel what could have become an entertainment empire. I will delve deeper into this topic later in the chapter. What's important to understand is the immeasurable impact of addiction—not just on the individual, but on families, legacies, and potential futures. It leaves behind a trail of *"what could have been"*—a regret that lingers long after the addiction ends.

I also had a personal crossroads moment. In 2020, after undergoing shoulder surgery, I firmly instructed my doctor not to prescribe opioids. Nevertheless, I awoke from surgery to find a bottle waiting at my bedside. I never touched it. Tylenol sufficed. Weeks later, while dropping off the medication at a pharmacy, the technician joked, *"Do you know how much this is worth on the street?"* I smiled politely, but inside, I knew the actual cost of addiction. It's not just measured in money—it's paid in relationships, mental health, and lost time.

I come from a family with strong addictive tendencies. I remember the first time I smoked a cigarette—it took me 20 years to quit. Alcohol and drugs were never my personal struggles, but I knew the damage they were capable of inflicting. I had seen that damage firsthand, and I refused to let it define me.

Intergenerational Addiction and Family Trauma

My father often spoke of his grandfather and uncle—both alcoholics who died prematurely as a result of their addictions. One of them, he believed, had frozen to death at a bus stop on Jefferson Avenue in Buffalo, New York. The details were murky, but the tragedy was unmistakable.

According to my father, his grandfather had traveled from Anniston, Alabama, seeking help from his son—my grandfather, a Church of God minister. Because of his father's alcoholism, my grandfather refused to let him stay in the house. Sometime later, Buffalo authorities allegedly informed my grandfather that his father had been found deceased on the street.

To confirm the story for this book, I spoke with my uncle—my father's younger brother. He clarified that it was actually their uncle, not their grandfather, who died in that tragic manner. Yet despite the inconsistency in the identity of the deceased, both my father and uncle recalled strikingly similar incidents: being tasked by their father to retrieve their father and uncle from bars across Buffalo due to their heavy drinking. My grandfather, it seems, was desperate to hide or contain the embarrassment of their behavior.

It's clear to me now that my grandfather was reliving his own trauma—inflicted by his father and uncle—and trying to shield his family from its corrosive effects. Still, trauma has a way of trickling through generations. Though he may have tried to suppress it, the pain my grandfather carried was inevitably passed down to my father and his siblings. The stories my father shared about his upbringing—stories of physical beatings and emotional torment—were difficult to comprehend.

What's ironic is that my personal memories of my grandfather are filled with warmth and love. He made sure I went to church every Sunday. I remember sitting beside him on Saturday nights, listening to tales from his youth. I cherished those moments. My father, to his credit, shielded me from the pain he had endured, allowing me to enjoy those good memories.

Perhaps my grandfather's tenderness toward my brother and me was his way of atoning for the way he had raised his own children. What I do know is that the trauma he suffered and inflicted didn't end with him. It shaped my father—and, in turn, shaped me and my siblings. Only near the end of his life did I begin to understand the root of my father's behavior.

I wish he had found healing sooner. I often reflect on the potential of what could have been—what our family might have looked like had addiction not loomed so large in our history. My father was a brilliant man, but his demons and unhealed trauma left lasting scars.

Looking back, it's clear that the trauma I've experienced—and that my children now feel, hopefully to a lesser extent—began long before my time. Possibly even before my great-grandfather. Addiction is generational. It's a curse that passes through families silently, but it can be broken. With love, prayer, self-awareness, and determination, that cycle can come to an end.

As I mentioned earlier, my brother has told his story in his own book, and soon I will do the same. My story in no way discounts my brother's account, but it does offer a different ending than may give fullness to a prior account. Before my father passed, he asked me for forgiveness. I gave it to him. That gave me a sense of closure, but not without lingering pain. The memories remain. They manifest in ways I interact with others and sometimes trigger responses that reopen old wounds—mine or theirs. Trauma is like rusty nails embedded in the foundation of our lives. When we stumble upon them, they can still cut deep.

Addiction is a ghost that haunts generations. You may not see it, but you feel its presence—in distrust, in fear, and in inherited behaviors. It takes courage to break that cycle. By sharing these stories, I hope to offer a map out of that darkness.

Balanced Responses to Addiction: *Lessons from Life and Teaching*

My upbringing was pivotal in shaping my beliefs about drug and alcohol abuse. Often, when responding to an addict, people take one of two extreme approaches: a harsh response, such as John Adams renouncing his son, or an enabling one. I've heard stories where addiction began when a teenager shared their first joint with a parent. Others have shared sentiments like, *"If my parents hadn't given me all that money, I probably would've stopped a lot sooner."* I've witnessed both behaviors—enabling and rejecting—and neither is the right answer.

As with many things in life, the right response lies somewhere in the middle. Above all, love must always be shown to someone battling addiction. That love can ignite hope, and from hope, recovery becomes possible. However, love must not take the form of enabling. Conversely, completely cutting off an addict can lead to devastating outcomes. How many addicts suffer on the streets due to the extreme reactions of loved ones? Sometimes, loved ones reach a breaking point, and understandably, they can no longer cope. Still, that should be a last resort—not the first response.

I once leaned toward the extreme. I could not tolerate seeing friends or family intoxicated. I remember telling my children that if they were ever arrested for drugs, I would not bail them out. In fact, I told them I would bail them out for murder before drugs—believing that at least with murder, there might have been a reason, such as self-defense. But with drugs, I saw no justification. That extreme stance created long-lasting consequences in my household—consequences still being healed today.

Everything changed when I was assigned to teach inmates in the Indiana Department of Corrections. Many of them reach out to tell me I changed their lives, but they don't realize how much they changed mine. Addiction is profoundly complicated.

My years spent teaching inmates preparing for reentry into society gave me one of the most unfiltered views of addiction's wrath. Many of these individuals committed crimes—burglary, fraud, violence—driven by desperation to sustain a habit. They lost everything: careers, families, homes, and even their sense of identity.

Yet, within those same prison walls, I witnessed transformation. I saw men and women reclaim their lives through education, faith, and community support. They reminded me that while addiction breaks, recovery rebuilds. Their stories reflect the central message of this book: recovery is real, and redemption is always possible.

Addiction Respects No Boundaries

Too often, addiction is mistakenly viewed as a "low-income issue" or something confined to urban settings. This is a dangerous and misleading misconception. I grew up in a quiet, suburban neighborhood just outside of Buffalo— quaint, tree-lined, and seemingly secure. Despite the appearance of safety, drugs and alcohol silently infiltrated our community, taking the lives of many of my childhood friends. One by one, they succumbed to overdoses, became incarcerated, or were consumed by despair.

Addiction is not a problem of geography. It is a human problem. It transcends socioeconomic status, location, and background. It invades every social layer, indiscriminately. In this way, addiction becomes the equalizer of pain—bringing suffering to people from all walks of life.

A Book of Recovery and Transformation

Stories of Transgression and Recovery stands apart from any other volume in the Stories Of series. These are not merely tales of hardship—they are profound narratives of survival, transformation, and strength. Each contributor has faced adversity head-on, endured the fire, and emerged resilient. These stories are raw, honest, and, most importantly, true.

This book was created to serve both as a testament and a tool. It is a testament to the indomitable resilience of the human spirit, and a practical guide for those still navigating the depths of addiction or dealing with the lasting impacts it leaves behind. Whether you are personally struggling or supporting someone who is, this book opens a window into what recovery can truly look like—and offers the hope that healing is always possible.

Conclusion: What to Do with This Book

After reading this book, I encourage you to do one of two things:

1. Pass it along to someone who may need it—a friend, a loved one, or even a stranger.
2. Keep it as a personal guide—a companion for those moments when summoning strength feels nearly impossible.

Addiction and trauma may not respect boundaries, but neither do hope and recovery. The stories contained within these pages are powerful proof of that truth.

Let this book remind you: You are not alone. Your story is not over. And the power to change is still within your grasp.

Trunnis Goggins II

runnis Goggins II, an accomplished educator, author, and consultant, hails from Buffalo, New York, and now resides in Asheville, North Carolina. With a distinguished military background, he's earned five Navy and Marine Corps Achievement Medals. Recognized by organizations such as NASPAA and NSLS, Trunnis has provided consulting services to small businesses nationwide and guided higher education institutions in accreditation and online learning initiatives. With over 16 years of experience in higher education, he has held roles such as professor, department chair, and director of workforce development. Currently, he serves as a lead instructor in the College of Business at Western Governors University, where he leverages his extensive experience to empower students with practical knowledge and skills essential for success in the ever-evolving business landscape.

The Story of

Ryan Mader

A Quiet Morning

I woke up this morning next to the most beautiful woman in the world—my wife, Chastidy. Sunlight poured through the window, casting a warm glow across the room. Outside, birds were singing.

To anyone else, it might've seemed like just another morning. But not to me. Because I'm not just here. I am alive. And I am living.

21

As I got up to make coffee, she stirred under the blankets, still wrapped in sleep. I looked around—books stacked on our desks, her stethoscope hanging from the doorknob, my notebook from the night before left open to a half-finished page. Small things. Quiet things. But together, they tell the story of a life we were fortunate enough to build.

Chastidy earned her master's last year and now works as a nurse practitioner—bringing the same strength and compassion that helped carry us through the darkest days.

And me? I work as a case manager at a recovery center, leading groups for men who are walking the same hard roads I once did. In a few months, I'll graduate with my associate's degree. Next year, I'll start working toward a dual master's in law and human services.

We live in a calm, clean loft in a part of town people want to be in. It's not flashy—but it's safe. Steady. And most of all, it is ours.

And this morning, standing in the soft light with coffee in my hand, I looked over at the woman I love sleeping nearby. I felt it all at once: What a miracle it is just to be here. And I wouldn't change a thing.

Foundations of Peace

I came into this world with a sense of normalcy. As a child, my mom and I lived with my grandparents. She worked and attended school, pursuing a degree in nursing. The first five years of my life were simple, stable, and safe.

I never knew my biological father and have never truly learned the cause of his absence. Still, I felt secure in the family I did have. My grandparents loved me deeply — especially my grandmother. I was a sensitive kid, often overwhelmed and tearful, but she always knew how to calm me.

They had a place on the White River in southern Indiana, near Spencer. We'd drive down from Indianapolis and spend weekends there. To me, it was the most peaceful place in the world. The quiet, the trees, the water — it all settled me. I got to spend time with my grandpa, my hero. We'd swim, fish, and sit around campfires listening to him tell stories.

My cousin Ron — a big brother to me — was around often, along with his parents, Aunt Donna, and Uncle Jeff. My cousin Sarah — more like a big sister — was also a constant, loving presence. Those days defined my sense of family and belonging.

That foundation made what came next even harder to reconcile. I had known what peace and love felt like, and the contrast between those early days and what followed would haunt me for years to come. Looking back, I see how deeply I depended on that calm. It left me unprepared for anything else.

The warmth of campfires, the rhythm of river weekends, and the steady presence of my grandparents gave way to a sharp turn I never could've prepared for. I had no idea those peaceful days would be eclipsed by something far more challenging to understand.

When I was around three or four years old, Jim came into our lives. My mom had met him, and he quickly became part of our world. At first, he was kind and dependable—everything I needed in a father figure. He took me fishing and tossed the football with me at the park. He was fun, and he made us happy. He didn't live with us right away, so life at my grandparents stayed the same. They seemed to like him, too.

By the time I was five, my mom married Jim. Not long after, we moved into a townhouse in a quiet neighborhood, and I started kindergarten. Around the same time, the first of my three younger brothers was born.

In the beginning, we were an all-American family. Jim helped with homework and took us to the movies. He brought a steadiness I didn't know I'd missed.

What none of us could understand or expect then was that Jim was approaching the age when schizophrenia begins to present. And once it did, everything changed.

I remember the day it showed up–like it was yesterday. We were sitting at the kitchen table, eating dinner—spaghetti and salad. Out of nowhere, Jim exploded, yelling at my mom. Then he punched her in the mouth and knocked her to the floor.

Before I could even process it, he turned and hit me in the side of the head. I flew out of my chair. My plate shattered against the wall. I can still hear the glass breaking, taste the blood in my mouth, and feel the cold linoleum against my cheek.

His fists kept coming. My mom's voice filled the room, screaming for him to stop. I saw him turn back toward her—then everything went quiet.

Afterward, I was sent to my room. I lay there in silence. I went to school the next day, and every movement hurt. My body ached, but the worst pain was inside. I didn't understand what had happened or why. I just remember being afraid.

That was the beginning.

The beatings became a regular part of life—sometimes two or three times a week—for the next eight years. Jim's delusions and hallucinations made him see my mom and me as enemies, part of some conspiracy against him. Once a place of warmth and security, our home was transformed overnight into a place of chaos and constant fear.

His abuse ebbed and flowed. For weeks at a time, the old Jim would reappear—gentle and kind, like nothing had ever happened. Then, just as suddenly, he'd vanish, and the violence would return. It wasn't always physical. Sometimes he screamed, accused, and degraded. He isolated us from my mom's family. And each time he calmed, we clung to hope that this time, he was back for good.

I found ways to escape—mostly through my imagination. I'd zone out in class, which led to poor grades and more beatings at home. By third grade, the school suspected a learning disability and sent me for IQ testing.

What they found shocked them—my IQ tested at 155. But brilliance meant nothing in a world where survival was the only subject.

I wasn't slow. I was in shock. But no one saw the correlation. I couldn't think clearly. I moved through each day bracing for the worst, disconnected from myself and everything around me. There wasn't space in my mind for hope—just the instinct to endure whatever came next.

After the testing, I was offered a chance to attend a program for gifted children. But Jim believed it was part of a government plot to brainwash me—another layer of his delusion. That door closed, and another never opened.

My mom, trapped in fear and the confusion of trauma, didn't fight him. Instead, she enrolled my brother and me in a local Catholic school at his insistence. On the surface, it probably seemed like a good choice—structured and safe. But to me, it was just another place I didn't belong.

I was thrown into a rigid environment where no one understood what I was dealing with at home—where my fear made it nearly impossible to focus on anything else.

Over the next few years, I became increasingly disconnected—not just from school, but from myself as well. At home, Jim's unpredictability kept me in a state of constant alert. At school, I was the kid who didn't turn in homework, stared out the window, and disappeared into his own head. I didn't make friends—or maybe I pushed people away without realizing it.

When I wasn't at school, I would walk or ride my bike for hours, just to be anywhere but home. I searched for quiet places, for a sense of safety—but it was the motion itself that felt safest.

Descent

By the time I was fifteen, I'd had enough. I started hanging out with the wrong crowd and numbing myself in any way I could. Weed and alcohol led to cocaine and other drugs. I started staying gone for weeks at a time—crashing at friends' houses, stealing cars at night, or committing other crimes to support an already unmanageable lifestyle.

Over the next eight years, I racked up arrest after arrest—non-violent crimes, minor drug charges, and thefts. It became an endless loop.

Get arrested. Get out. Get high. Get arrested again. I was on a carousel of chaos.

And right in the middle of that chaos—my daughter Haley was born. By then, I wasn't simply able to quit.

Even if I'd wanted to change, there wasn't a track out. I was a passenger on a runaway train—long past the point of slowing down. I wasn't just slinging a little dope on the side anymore. I was involved with people whose business model was built on volume, speed, and pressure.

I'd get fifty thousand dollars' worth of meth on consignment. And before the last batch was gone—or even paid off—another drop would land in my lap. I was never caught up. Never clear. Never free to walk away.

I knew I was supposed to feel something when Haley was born—joy, purpose, maybe even fear. But what I felt most was a sense of being trapped. Trapped between what I was doing, who I was becoming, and what I knew I'd never be able to give her.

Still, I remember seeing her in the hospital for the first time—how perfect she was, how tiny and pure. And how completely undeserving I felt. For the first time in my life, I felt something close to clarity: I wanted to be the man she needed. I just didn't know how.

I told myself I'd fix it later—when things calmed down.

But things never did. And in the end, I left her behind before I ever had the chance to be there.

Suddenly, everything came to a screeching halt.

It was July 2003. I was twenty-five when the weight of the U.S. government bore down on me. I was indicted in federal court for trafficking methamphetamine.

This time, I wasn't getting right back out. I was facing some serious time—and I got it: a thirteen-year sentence.

You might think thirteen years in the federal system would be enough to turn someone's life around. Maybe for some, it serves as that 'rock bottom.' But I stayed defiant. I hadn't suffered enough to convince myself that change was necessary.

Federal prison wasn't a wall I crashed into. It was just the next stretch of track after leaving the switchyard. After the shock of sentencing, the train started moving again—but it wasn't headed anywhere new. It just slid into darkness.

I didn't want to change. I spent my time gambling— betting on football, playing poker—and using whatever I could get my hands on: meth, Suboxone, psych meds. Throughout my stay, some form of mind-altering chemical coursed through my veins.

I even taught myself the law—how to file habeas petitions, how to craft §1983 civil rights complaints. I got good at it, too. Good enough guys would pay me to write their writs or explain cases to them.

But I wasn't doing it to fight for justice or better myself. I was doing it to make money—to buy drugs, to gamble, to keep the hustle alive from inside the fence.

Federal prison was just a tunnel the train passed through.

In 2014, I walked out of prison—but not as a free man. I walked out with a full-blown heroin habit and a belief system that hadn't changed one bit. If anything, it had hardened.

For a while, I managed to get by on Suboxone. It wasn't detectable on the standard tests used by probation, so I flew under the radar. I got a job, bought a truck, and saved a few thousand dollars. On the surface, it looked like I was doing better.

But even maintenance wore thin. I got tired of mediocrity. I wanted to get high.

Eventually, I went back to meth and heroin. Within weeks, the job was gone. The truck was gone. The money was gone. I picked up right where I'd left off—using and dealing to support my habit. I began circling the drain—again.

Collision and Grace

That's when I met Chastidy.

Yes, we met in full-blown addiction.

It was love at first sight for me—and she said it was the same for her. There was something about her that reached a place in me I thought was long gone. She was the only person outside of my family I ever truly cared about—someone I loved just as much as the drugs.

She brought warmth into my cold world. A warmth I hadn't felt since before the darkness eclipsed my life.

Her story mirrored mine. She hadn't been in the game as long, but addiction had taken just as much. Like so many, she started with OxyContin, which led to heroin. And heroin took everything—her job as a nurse, her home, her kids.

But even in her brokenness, she carried something I didn't: **faith**.

She talked to me about Jesus. About redemption. About God's unconditional love for people like us. She prayed for us daily, begged God to break the chains of our addictions, and carried a Bible everywhere. She believed in something better—even when I couldn't believe in myself.

A couple of months after we met, I got arrested on a state drug charge. I made bond, but it violated my federal supervised release. The judge ordered me into long-term inpatient treatment, promising leniency if I completed the program.

I agreed—but only to get out. I didn't want to get clean.

I lasted a couple of weeks before I got high again. And once I did, I ran.

I left the treatment center and took off with Chastidy. I didn't care what kind of trouble it put me in. I just knew I didn't want to lose her—and I wasn't ready to face life without being high.

She had state charges, too—enough to put a warrant out under her name. So we were both running. Both wanted.

Constantly using, never staying in one place long, always looking over our shoulders.

We were running on fumes—emotionally and physically.

Then one day, she told me she was done.

She said she couldn't keep living the way we were. That she was going to turn herself in, get clean, and go back to being a mother. She told me it could be a long time before we talked again—maybe not until her kids were grown.

She said it calmly. Clearly. Not with anger or blame—but with love.

And I felt the pain rise up and do what it always did: overwhelm me. I panicked. I couldn't sit with it. I couldn't face it.

So I did what I always did.

I ran.

We stopped at a gas station. She went inside. I drove off.

I didn't even know why—I just knew I couldn't stay.

I drove around for a while. I had been up for days—spun out, exhausted, broken in a way I couldn't yet name. I parked and passed out behind the wheel.

When I came to, the panic hit. I didn't want our last moment to be me leaving.

I went back to find her, but she was gone.

What I didn't know was that she had already done the hard thing. She had walked—alone—all the way to the jail and turned herself in.

Later that day, I got pulled over. I gave a fake name. The cop knew better.

He ran me and found the federal warrant.

I should've been taken straight to the Marshals or the sheriff's department. But instead, I was dropped off at the county processing center.

The jail staff realized the mistake after the arresting officer left. They said they'd hold me until they figured out what to do.

As I was being led to a holding cell, I heard someone call out a last name.

It was Chastidy's.

She stepped out from another cell. Her eyes were swollen from crying.

We locked eyes.

And then, without hesitation, we both said it—at the exact same time:

"I love you."

It wasn't a reunion. It wasn't a rescue.

It was a goodbye.

For both of us, it was the moment we needed — to let go and face what was next.

We were about to take two different paths — toward recovery, toward redemption. And I thank God for giving us that last moment to say goodbye and watch each other take those first steps.

Two days later, I stood before the Honorable Judge Larry McKinney in the United States District Court. I was sentenced to 27 months for violating my supervised release.

Before handing down the sentence, he looked at me and said something I've never forgotten:

"I see a man standing in front of me with endless potential. A man who could have a meaningful and purposeful life — if only he could learn to love himself."

At the time, I didn't believe him. I didn't understand what he saw in me. But his words never left me.

I went back into the federal system. I tried to stay clean — not because I was ready for recovery, but because I wanted Chastidy to be proud of me. I still held onto the hope that we'd find our way back to each other.

For two years, I didn't use drugs—except for the antidepressants prescribed by the prison doctor. I ate healthily. I worked out every day. I came out in the best physical shape of my life.

But my mind and spirit were still in shambles.

Everything I did—the clean time, the workouts, the diet—was about appearances. I looked changed, but I wasn't. I hadn't faced the truth about myself or the damage I had caused.

So it didn't take long to fall back into old patterns.

Meanwhile, Chastidy was out there building a new life. She was sober. Enrolled in college. Rebuilding her relationship with her kids.

She was doing the work I still couldn't fully commit to.

The Mirror and the Mountain

After I was released from the 27-month federal sentence, the state imposed a lengthy term of probation on the original drug charge that had triggered my supervised release violation. Over the next 18 months, I failed drug tests, missed appointments, and picked up new charges. The court gave me more chances than I deserved—and I wasted all of them.

Eventually, my probation was revoked, and I was given a nine-year sentence. That's when I finally hit rock bottom. By then, arrests, jail cells, and prison sentences had become so routine that you could have said I was institutionalized—and you'd have been right.

But that morning, it was all different. The day after receiving the nine-year sentence, I woke up in my cell in a panic.

It occurred to me that I was forty years old—and had nothing but a cement cage to show for nearly half a century on this planet. I started thinking about the last twenty years of my life. The years seemed to have clicked by in the mere snap of a finger. I couldn't account for the time. I couldn't explain where it went. And I found that realization terrifying.

But what startled me most was the mirror.

When I looked in it, I didn't recognize the man staring back at me.

He was a stranger.

The man looking back appeared old, tired, emotionally exhausted, and in a state of profound disconnect. If that man was me, then I didn't want to be him anymore.

I wanted to ask the gaunt figure in the mirror: Where did the time go? What did you do with it? Where are you headed? Is this what you want for the rest of your life? And if not... what can you do right now to change it?

These questions dominated my conscious thoughts and followed me into my sleep. I began to take an inventory of the last twenty-six years. And what I found was difficult to accept — but it was the undeniable truth.

I had sunk to the lowest levels imaginable. I saw the wake of destruction I had left behind — the pain I had caused everyone close to me. My mother. My grandparents. My daughter. My family. All of them had carried the burden of my addiction.

And I had failed them. Completely.

Addiction had made me a liar, a cheater, and a thief. The man in the mirror wasn't just tired — he was morally bankrupt and spiritually hollow. I pitied him. I hated him. I felt repulsed by him.

And I realized something else: For over a quarter century, I'd been trying to outrun that man. Every arrest. Every relapse. Every lie. It was all an attempt to escape the truth of who I had become.

But running hadn't worked. So if I couldn't escape that man... I would have to change him. For good.

Right there, in that cell, staring at my own reflection, I made a decision: I was done with addiction. I was done destroying myself and everyone around me. I decided, then and there, to never use drugs again. And I haven't since.

I didn't walk out of that moment in the mirror as a changed man. However, I did walk out of it with a changed mindset.

Something shifted after I made the decision to stop running. I didn't know exactly what change would look like, or how long it would take—but I knew I couldn't keep living by the same code that had guided me for decades. I had to start thinking differently. To do that, I had to start seeing things differently.

That's when I turned to writing.

At first, it was just a way to get the noise out of my head. I jotted and scribbled. The thoughts spilled out—messy, chaotic, disconnected. It was frustrating not to be able to make sense of the mess in my mind, but at least it was out of me and on the page.

I was determined to figure out how to say what I was thinking—what I was feeling. But no matter how hard I tried, I couldn't seem to get it right. I'd start a thought and lose it halfway through. I'd write a sentence that felt true, then scratch it out because it sounded wrong. It was like trying to hold water in my hands—everything kept slipping through.

Still, I kept showing up. Page after page. Some days it was just a few broken lines. On other days, it was pages of scattered emotion. And little by little, it started to change.

The page slowed me down. It gave me space to breathe, to reflect. Slowly, I began to work on making sense of what I'd written—organizing it, connecting the pieces, and confronting the ideas.

Writing didn't just help me express what I felt—it made me examine why I felt it. It became a way to interrogate the logic behind my pain, the justifications I'd built over the years, and the belief system that had carried me from trauma to destruction again and again. The act of writing gave shape to things I had only ever reacted to.

In April 2020, I entered the PLUS program—a yearlong, faith-based character development course inside IDOC. That's when the writing deepened. Each week, we were asked to reflect on themes like responsibility, humility, anger, and faith. But I wasn't just completing assignments—I was examining myself. I wasn't journaling to survive anymore. I was writing to dissect, to challenge, and ultimately, to rebuild.

I wrote appellate-style arguments—against my own thinking. Against the worldview I'd clung to for decades. I challenged the stories I used to justify the life I'd lived. I asked myself in these written briefs: Was I too damaged to change? Did my pain excuse the destruction I caused? Was I a victim of circumstance—or a product of my own choices?

The more I wrote, the more I questioned. And the more I questioned, the more I uncovered.

Through that process, something even deeper began to happen. My writing didn't just lead me inward—it pointed me upward. That intense scrutiny created space for a clarity I hadn't felt in years. And in that clarity, I found myself opening back up to the idea of a higher power.

For the first time in a long time, I let God back into my life.

I realized I didn't have to carry everything alone. I turned my life over to God—and from that point on, faith became a foundation, not just a concept.

I began to realize how many of my choices were based on beliefs I had never thoroughly examined. I started to recognize the lies I had internalized—the ones that let me off the hook, that kept me angry, guarded, and numb.

Writing became the place where I told the truth. Sometimes, for the first time.

One of the most pivotal shifts came in how I saw my mother. For years, I carried a quiet, bitter resentment—for not protecting me from Jim, for not leaving sooner, for the silence that followed. But through the trauma materials in the PLUS program, and by applying the same process I was using in my writing, those feelings began to dissolve. I started to understand the psychological weight of trauma and how paralyzing abuse can be. I began to see that she wasn't just a bystander—she was a prisoner too. Especially in the 1980s culture, escape wasn't simple. Our society lacked the resources it has now to help women like her. She hadn't failed me. She had survived—just like I was trying to. That realization broke something open in me. Not anger. Compassion.

By April 2021, I had completed the PLUS program. But I wasn't done. I stayed on as a facilitator, mentoring other men and helping them use the same tools that had changed my life. I kept writing, kept questioning, and kept applying what I'd learned. Recovery wasn't just abstaining from drugs anymore—it was the pursuit of clarity, character, and peace.

Then, in March 2023, I was granted a sentence modification and released—early and without probation. I had no home, no job, no formal reentry plan. I was dropped off at the Wheeler Mission in Bloomington, Indiana, with a duffel bag, a few hundred dollars, and a mindset I refused to lose.

I enrolled at Ivy Tech and began working toward my associate's degree. I got hired as a behavioral health technician at a treatment center. One of my coworkers offered me a room in the sober living house he managed, and I moved in within days. That became home for the next six months.

In January 2024, I joined two others from the community to help Vietnam veteran Stewart Eaton, who had been living in his car in the driveway of his home—destroyed by fire three years earlier. The Bloomington Herald-Times picked up the story, and it soon gained traction. People Magazine ran a feature, and offers of support and assistance poured in. Within a month, we decided to move forward with building him a new house, relying on volunteers and funds raised through donations.

In April 2024, I was elected to the Board of Directors for New Leaf New Life, a nonprofit organization dedicated to supporting individuals impacted by incarceration and promoting successful reentry into the community. In my role, I help guide program development, advocate for policy reforms, and ensure that our services meet the needs of those transitioning from the criminal justice system. Our mission centers around dignity, second chances, and reducing recidivism through practical support and human connection.

Also in April 2024, out of the blue, I got a message from Chastidy. Even though she had always held a place in my heart and soul, I had long accepted that we might never speak again. So when she reached out and asked if I wanted to meet for lunch, I was more than surprised. I was ecstatic. Later that month, Chastidy graduated from Indiana Wesleyan University with a master's in nursing science.

Not long after, Chastidy and I moved into an apartment together.

A few months later, she passed board certifications and began working as a Nurse Practitioner.

In March 2025, Stewart Eaton's house was complete, and he was able to sleep in his own bed for the first time in over four years.

A year after reuniting, on April 7, 2025, we were married on Venice Beach, Florida.

Ryan Mader

Ryan Mader is a writer, case manager, and advocate for recovery and reentry. After overcoming decades of addiction, incarceration, and personal trauma, Ryan has transformed his life through faith, writing, and service to others. He currently works at a recovery center, leading support groups for men navigating the same struggles he once endured. A passionate student, Ryan is completing his associate's degree and plans to pursue a dual master's in law and human services.

Ryan's writing has become both a personal lifeline and a public platform for redemption. His memoir, Transgression and Recovery, traces his powerful journey from trauma to transformation. He serves on the board of New Leaf New Life, a nonprofit supporting individuals impacted by incarceration, and played a key role in a nationally recognized project to rebuild a home for a homeless veteran.

Ryan lives in Indiana with his wife, Chastidy—his partner in both recovery and faith.

The Story of

Scott Free

It's the **"strangest feeling"** to write this story down after having told *it "So many times with so many different people"*. The emotions from these events have changed from when they were happening to where I am right now. I've changed the names to protect everyone involved and am not writing this to hurt anyone. I also admit that I'm not innocent in all the events that took place. With the tools I have now and a better understanding of addiction, I realize my actions were due to an inability to cope with events as they happened and after.

The story begins in 2013 when my first marriage was in a difficult place. My ex-wife and I were struggling financially after losing a significant amount of money on a house sale. We had a young daughter, but the strain on our relationship was immense, and it eventually ended. I met my ex-wife shortly after losing both my parents, and her family had *"taken me in as one of theirs"*.

After my divorce in 2013, I spent a significant amount of time attending promotional events for a beer company as part of my job as a radio host. It was at these events that I met a young woman whom, for the sake of this story, we will call **"Anna"**, a promotions girl for the company. I was drawn to her organized and "**put-together**" nature. I was in a poor emotional state, and with Anna's attention, one thing led to another, and we eventually became a couple. The appeal of a younger woman who was desired by many men but paid attention to me was a "**rush**". Soon after we started our relationship, we moved in together, and she became pregnant very quickly.

Red Flags and Rising Tensions

Early in our relationship, Anna and I would often go to different bars. I never suspected any issues; I just thought she *"really liked to have a good time"* and could *"hold her alcohol"*. However, a couple of things surfaced that I didn't pay attention to at the time. One evening at her family's home, her mother looked at me and said, *"You know, she acts like she has the brain of a teenager"*. I didn't know what that meant and blew it off, thinking they just had *"past issues"*. I later learned from Anna that both her grandfathers and her father were alcoholics, but at the time, I thought that didn't automatically make her one.

I now know that Al-Anon calls alcoholism a *"family disease"* because it affects the *"whole family"*. Anna never told me she struggled with alcohol; that didn't come out until much later. I began to notice that Anna would complain of being **"sick,"** which I now realize was her *"hiding bottles and drinking to the point of passing out"*. At the time, I was in denial and didn't have the tools to know what to do. I learned that alcoholism is a *"progressive disease,"* and it only got worse. Anna's drinking cycle involved benders lasting a day or two before starting again.

By November 2013, Anna was pregnant, but she *"couldn't stop drinking"*. After multiple emergency room visits, she, her father, and I drove her to a very expensive inpatient treatment center, where she decided to stay. I would drive eight hours every Sunday for a two-hour visit. Toward the end of the 30-day treatment, the staff suggested Anna stay until the baby was born, but she wanted to go home and have a *"normal pregnancy"*. I was hopeful, thinking the treatment must have worked.

A Father's Shame and a Child's Protection

I carry *"a lot of shame and guilt"* for what happened to my daughter from my first marriage. After her mother and I separated, my daughter moved to Cleveland, Ohio, while I stayed in New York for my job. I initially saw her every couple of weeks, but as Anna's problems continued, I saw my daughter less and less. I didn't want my oldest daughter to see what was happening, and every time I planned a visit, Anna would get drunk and *"make that trip about her"*.

I recall a visit when my daughter was around 10 or 11 years old. When we returned home to leave, we found Anna passed out at the top of the stairs. I immediately tried to shelter my daughter from seeing it, telling her to stay downstairs while I got her bag. I called Anna's father to come *"tend to Anna"* while I drove my daughter home. I didn't want my daughter to see those things or have to explain them to her because she was very young and impressionable. I acknowledge that I wasn't there when I should have been and have not had the opportunity to talk to my oldest daughter about it because she has chosen not to have contact with me at this time. My oldest daughter is now a strong, well-educated young woman.

A Cycle of Hope and Despair

A week after returning from inpatient treatment, Anna drank herself unconscious and was taken to the hospital again. The treatment center offered to help, but it was too expensive, and Anna did not want to return. I realized then that she wanted to drink and not get better. Despite this, she carried the baby to term and delivered.

After our son was born, Anna started drinking again, citing frustration from not being able to breastfeed and the strains of being a new mom. One day, her texts became incoherent and then stopped altogether, and I received a call from the New York State Troopers, instructing me to come home. I arrived to find Trooper and Child Protective Services (CPS) cars in my driveway. Anna was arrested for criminal neglect and child abuse. I discovered that Anna's own mother had called CPS, thinking they would **help** with Anna's addiction and care for the baby. A plan was made to ensure Anna would not be alone with our son.

Just before the CPS case was set to close, Anna, on her way back from a trip to Canada, was pulled over for erratic driving. In a panic, I went and picked her up, filled with anger that we were so close to getting the court out of our lives.

A Spiraling Descent and Tough Choices

The day after Anna's DUI, I received a phone call from the CPS agent, and I was furious. I went into panic mode and made a series of poor choices. Anna promised she wouldn't drink, but she did. One day, a friend found her unconscious in one of the living rooms, and our son was crawling around with a full diaper and crying. The friend took our son and called CPS.

Angry and feeling helpless, I called Anna's father, who had moved to North Carolina, and we made a plan for me to fly our son there to get my son out of reach of Child Protective Services. I dreaded the thought of our son being placed in foster care and the **personal** embarrassment that would come with it. I even asked a daycare provider to lie for me. Upon my return, I was arrested for lying to the police, but the charges were eventually dropped.

I admit I was too weak to tell Anna to leave and was still clinging to "**hope**" for the sake of thinking we needed to have the picture-perfect family. The court granted temporary custody to Anna's parents. I also had neglect charges brought against me by the CPS agent. During my trial, the judge found me to have neglected our son, even though I was at work. This sent me emotionally and mentally over the edge, and I began to despise Anna and her drinking. I didn't have the tools from therapy or Al-Anon to deal with it at the time.

A Fresh Start, a New Home, and a Repeating Pattern

In 2016, Anna and I moved to a new county for a *fresh start*. The house was strictly in my name, and I paid for everything. Anna did odd jobs, but nothing of a career level. I grew to resent carrying the financial load while Anna spent money on anything she pleased.

In 2017, we petitioned the court to regain custody of our son. While Anna's mother was in Europe, her father, who was also an alcoholic, relapsed. Anna drove to North

Carolina and found him passed out with our son, now almost four, in a full diaper and surrounded by broken glass. I met her halfway and took our son home; the judge then granted us custody again. I was once again caught up in **hope**.

However, I was still carrying a lot of resentment. I would tell Anna that she needed to *"get a real job,"* and I would sometimes struggle to hear her points, thinking, *"You sound like an entitled bitch"*. I noticed a pattern: if either Anna or her father relapsed, the other one would soon after. I also realized that Anna's mother was a **master manipulator** who was codependent on her husband and daughter's addiction.

The Final Collapse and a New Beginning

In 2019, Anna gave birth to our daughter. The drinking during this pregnancy was not as bad as with our son's. In 2021, Anna demanded that I put her name on the house title. I *buckled* to keep the peace, and we added her name to the title, even though I still paid for everything. Anna started working in food delivery and would often come home with a pretty powerful alcoholic beverage.

Late in 2021, things got bad again. I had done *all the wrong things*, like threatening to take her car keys, which I learned doesn't work. One evening, an intoxicated and belligerent Anna physically lunged at me. She fell into a kiddie pool and, at another point, fell and fractured a couple of fingers. The police were called, and I explained that I was *"trying to get her to go to bed to sleep it off"*. Anna gave multiple different stories to medical providers, none of which included a physical altercation. I later learned that she had filed a police report nearly a year later, inventing a story but also saying, *"Scott has never been abusive to the kids"*.

In 2022, Anna's mother moved to New York. Her father, without his wife's codependency, began drinking again. I noticed the pattern of one's relapse leading to the other's. In early 2022, Anna got her bachelor's degree and was hired for a good job, but just before her start date, she went on a bender. In a moment I'm not proud of, I lied to the company and told them Anna had COVID so she could postpone her start date. She did eventually start, but after a month or two, she would continue her food delivery job to buy the strong alcoholic beverages.

In June 2022, Anna was on a bender again and had to go to the hospital after drinking rubbing alcohol. A social worker contacted CPS again after Anna said, *"I just want to go home to my babies"*. Anna's mother was living locally, so we made arrangements with CPS for her to watch the kids while I was at work. Anna eventually had to go to a behavioral sciences unit and then to inpatient treatment again. Her job kept her employed and paid for the treatment. She was kicked out after 15 days for causing problems for the staff. The facility even took her to a train station right across from a liquor store.

In August 2022, Anna drank heavily while I was at a work event. I returned home at 9 p.m. to find her passed out, with our daughter lying next to her with an empty baby bottle. I immediately called her parents, explaining that I had to get the kids to them so I could get Anna help. I took time off from work and drove the kids to North Carolina. During the drive, Anna's mother suggested she go to a 6-month inpatient program in their native country, and the kids stay with them. I agreed, not realizing this was the beginning of a *master manipulation plan*.

After I dropped the kids off, Anna checked herself out of the hospital, took a rideshare home, and ordered more alcohol. I returned to find her passed out again. Her father suggested we get her to North Carolina for detox. I drove her 16 hours, stopping multiple times for her to be sick or urinate. The clinic even suggested giving her a beer to prevent alcohol withdrawal. At the end of the trip, Anna apologized for the first and only time. I now believe she may have attempted suicide by alcohol.

The Final Collapse and a New Beginning

Anna's mother suggested the kids stay in North Carolina for a few months while Anna *"gets things back together"*. I agreed, and Anna did a 30-day inpatient treatment in North Carolina. The plan was for the family to be back together by Christmas. However, Anna was sending signals that she didn't have plans to return with the kids. In April 2023, while at her parents' house, my daughter accidentally knocked over Anna's wallet, and I saw a card for an attorney. The day I had my conference with the attorney, I received a certified letter from Anna suing me for custody of the children. I was irate and couldn't believe she was doing a custody grab. My attorney advised me to go to North Carolina without telling Anna and petition to have the case heard in New York. I was blown away to see in the court papers that Anna had lied about there being no previous cases.

Anna's attorney didn't show up to the hearing, not believing the case would be moved from North Carolina to New York. Anna had weaved a story to her attorney about all sorts of abuse. I learned that it's not uncommon for addicts, especially female addicts, to blame someone else and use abuse as an excuse to garner sympathy. The North

Carolina judge ultimately said she would discuss the case with a New York judge. I stayed in North Carolina and texted Anna that I was in town and wanted to see the kids. She agreed, but only if her father escorted them. I realized her entire family was enabling her.

On my way back to New York, my attorney called and said, *"Anna has filed a domestic violence order against you and an order of protection"*.

I was in disbelief and broke down, asking, *"How, why, what does this mean?"*.

At the hearing, I watched Anna weave a story using crocodile tears and invent situations. She had secretly recorded me during arguments and would play snippets to the judge. I didn't realize it at the time, but the judge was playing Anna and knew she was lying.

When the judge asked when she decided not to return to New York, Anna's answer, which was the Christmas of this year, sealed the case's fate because the timeline didn't match the residency requirement.

A temporary order came down for the kids to come home with me for a summer visit. By the end of August, another order came that the kids were to remain in New York. The full trial was a day and a half long in October

2023. I watched Anna's mother exaggerate or create scenarios to make me look a certain way. Anna launched an all-out barrage against me numerous times. I was exhausted after the trial and realized I had been manipulated. I started attending weekly Al-Anon meetings in early 2023. I found an invaluable therapist.

In December 2023, the final order was issued, and I became the primary custodial parent, with the kids remaining in New York. I had also met someone and started a new relationship. My significant other has been a dose of reality, telling me I should have left after the first CPS case. I've learned the Al-Anon slogan, *"You didn't cause it, you can't control it, and you can't cure it,"* and I admit I tried to do the latter two and failed miserably.

In late 2024, our son was diagnosed with all five criteria for Fetal Alcohol Syndrome after falling behind in school. His mother still wants to deny the results and his need for ADHD medication. My daughter is healthy and may have been spared from what our son is going to have to live with.

In closing, I wish I were stronger and could have walked away sooner. I didn't understand the disease of alcoholism or that it was a *"family disease"* on so many levels. I don't hate Anna, but I hate what she continues to do, like continued denial and finger-pointing. I don't even feel that

I'm in a co-parenting situation, but I'll take care of things because that's what I have to do. I am thankful for my new significant other, who has been a wonderful partner and has given the kids a normal life. I also hope to reconcile with my oldest daughter and want her to know I love her very much. I advise others to **keep your eyes and ears** open and **take action for yourself and the ones closest to you that you love**.

Scott Free

S cott Free is the lively on-air personality behind The Scott and Ally Show, where unpredictability, energy, and laughter are always guaranteed. Known for *"going for the fun every time,"* Scott thrives on keeping things spontaneous—even when they get a little crazy.

His style is all about connection. Whether it's through live calls, constant texts, or buzzing social media interactions filled with behind-the-scenes moments, Scott makes sure listeners feel like part of the show. For him, the best part of radio is simple: knowing people choose to spend part of their day with him and Ally, sharing laughs, stories, and unforgettable moments.

THE STORY OF

DARCY K FREDERICK

Heavenly Outcast

There has never been a person whose life goal was to become an addict. I know, because I used to be one.

Living as a homeless teen on the streets of Minneapolis in the mid-1970s was a reality no one should have to face. Didn't know where I was going, what I would eat, or where I would sleep. I was scared most of the time and cried all of the time. Gas station bathrooms became my unexpected sanctuary. A safe place to sleep. At that time, most gas stations had bathrooms located outside the building, and sometimes they were left unlocked. I breathed a huge sigh of relief when I found one; otherwise, I would have had to stay up all night, and that meant risking everything. There was a constant fear that someone would hurt or kill me while I was sleeping. When you are a young girl living on the streets, you become prey. It's disturbing how many people can befriend you and assault you within the same hour.

One afternoon, I met up with a girl I knew from school who also had a hard life, and that day we made a pact to kill ourselves. We swallowed a full bottle of pain pills and used a razor knife to cut ourselves so we would bleed to death. For me, this resulted in 75 stitches from elbow to wrist, my arm in bandages, and a painful wound. It made living on the street harder than ever. One day, the stitches were starting to become one with my skin, so I had to find a way to remove them. I believe it was a local store where I borrowed scissors, and then I proceeded to cut each of the stitches out. Within a week, the wound split apart, and I was left with a long purple scar that was very painful to the touch. This was not the first time I tried to commit suicide, in fact, it was on my mind most of the time.

Many men would approach me on the street, but one man in particular said he wanted to help me. He gave me his phone number, and after several weeks, I decided to call him. He brought me to the basement of a house and that is where I lived for a while. One evening he dropped me off at a bar in downtown Minneapolis and told me to go in and talk to the boss. Two days later, I became a stripper at age 15. When I first started, I noticed all the other dancers were much older than I. Everything that could happen, did happen at this bar. One of the co-owners was shot and killed in the men's bathroom, and it was rumored that my boss hired someone to do it. The women's dressing room was right next to the office, and the walls were quite thin. We heard many conversations that took place in that office, and they were never good. There were corrupt police officers who came in regularly, and many times, I would hear the boss bragging about something awful he had done the day before. If I ever met someone with no heart, it was my boss, Kurt.

Part of working at the bar meant we had to sell champagne to the men and sit with them while they drank it. The servers would give us a chaser cup with a bit of soda and ice in it. This was so we could drink some champagne and take a drink from the chaser cup. What we were supposed to do was spit the champagne out into the cup so we wouldn't get drunk, but many times we would drink it instead. Drinking, smoking weed, and snorting cocaine made getting on the stage a little easier. You see, I couldn't stand dancing in front of a bar full of men, so I would get high and lost in the music.

It was at this time that my boyfriend started to get extremely violent. He would always say, *"This will make you stronger."* Often, I was covered with cuts and bruises, and then one day I started to fight back, which only made it worse. One night, he threw me down a flight of cement stairs, and I hit my head on the corner of the last step. Everything happened so fast, and I couldn't see anything, but I could feel the warm blood pouring out of my head and into my eyes. Then I felt someone pick me up by my hair, drag me outside, and begin slamming my head into the side of a car. I was crying, and at the same time, I was thinking of my family. I wanted so much to talk to someone in my family. I begged him to drop me off at the hospital, so he drove with one hand on the steering wheel while the other fist was punching me. As he pulled up to the Emergency Room door he whispered, *"Don't tell anyone who did this."*

The nurses took one look at me and called the police, who came and questioned me as the doctor put the stitches in. I told them I was jumped by someone downtown and didn't know who it was. They knew I was lying and told me I needed to tell them who did this to me, but I didn't. After the doctor was finished, they got me up, and as I walked past a mirror, I didn't know it was me. My eyes were so swollen that I could barely open one eye slightly. There were punch marks on my chest, legs, arms, and back. The right side of my head was shaved and there was a long row of stitches. This would turn out to be one of the many times something like this happened. It was common for me to wear something on my head and put a shawl over my shoulders to cover the remnants of the beating from the night before. The owner of the bar told me they would not allow me to dance like that and made me go home. This meant I had to go out on the street to get money, and it was one of the many low points in my life. I was afraid that if I got into someone's car, they would kill me. There was a change in me now. Like the sweetness of a child was fading away, and now I was just surviving. Sometimes I would wonder where God was.

My boyfriend was not a normal kind of boyfriend. He was a pimp and had many women that worked for him. In the 1970's, many pimps would bring several of their women to the bar and it was like a show. A competition to see which of the pimps had the prettiest and the most women in their **'stable'**. Some of the women were short term, some were long term. Just like a job. I was always hearing horror stories of what happened to some of the women who refused to do something their pimp instructed them to do. We were not allowed to look at another pimp in the face or that automatically meant you wanted to be with him. If one of us accidentally glanced in the direction of another pimp, we were taken outside and let me tell you, we never wanted to be taken outside.

A couple of years passed, and when I was about 17 years old, one night after I got home from working at the bar, I was in the basement of the house we lived in, and my boyfriend was getting ready to go out.

I asked if I could go with him, and he said in a sharp voice, "*No!.*"

Five minutes after he left, someone called on the telephone. It was a woman who said, *"Oh Darcy, you are all alone, aren't you?"*

I hung up the phone, and a few minutes later, I heard a noise upstairs and then the sound of people running down the basement stairs. Before I knew it, I could feel several punches to the face, someone kicking me in the middle of my back, and then something I will never forget. I felt someone grab me by the arm and bite me so hard, I saw stars. This was set up by my boyfriend, who had been seeing another woman for quite a while. He let her in the house with her friend so they could beat the living heck out of me. And that is what they did. It took weeks for me to recover, and again, I was unrecognizable. I have that bite mark on my arm to this day.

I was now living in another world. I took any drug that would prevent me from feeling anything: pain pills, weed, cocaine, acid, angel dust, and liquor. I did not want to live anymore. I hoped that I did not wake up the next day. I would cry at night in bed, asking Jesus to please hold me. I didn't understand why I was ever put on this planet. I couldn't take it anymore. One day, I looked in my boyfriend's glove compartment and found a small gun, and I made up my mind to kill myself. I sat for hours with the gun up to my head and my finger on the trigger. I have no idea why I didn't pull the trigger that night. It would have been so easy to end it all. One thing it did was wake me up and realize that I had to get away from this man before he drove me crazy or killed me.

Now I am 21 years old and pregnant. I found myself an apartment so I could get out of that basement and away from my boyfriend. I lived alone with a baby in my belly and a cat named Princess. It felt so good to be pregnant, drug free and away from that man. It was also the first time I had a home of my own. I woke up in the middle of the night at 3:00 am and thought I had wet the bed, but actually, it was my water that broke. I felt peaceful but didn't know who I could call for help. Since I couldn't think of anyone else, I called a taxicab. I stood by the window so I wouldn't miss the cab because back then, they only waited a couple of minutes before pulling off.

When it arrived, I went downstairs, got into the cab, and the man asked where I was going. I said, *"Abbott Hospital"*.

He started the meter, and we talked a little bit on the way.

When we got close, he said, *"Which door do you want to be dropped off at?"*

I said, *"The emergency door."*

He said, *"Are you picking someone up?"*

I said, *"No, I am dropping someone off."*

Then his expression changed, and he said, *"Are you having that baby?"*

I responded, *"Yes."*

He said, *"It's a good thing you didn't tell me, because I wouldn't have picked you up."*

No matter how many times I was told how bad labor pains were, I didn't expect this. I never heard of an epidural or had any drugs to help with the pain. I just went through it. I was in shock as to how any woman could live through this kind of pain. The time spent in the hospital with my baby was sweet, peaceful and safe.

A few months after my daughter was born, my older sister got in touch with me and came to visit. I was exhausted from being up all night with the baby so when my sister offered to help for a few days, I did not turn it down. My sister had a husband and four kids, and they were all excited to see my daughter. I got some sleep for the first time in months, had some dinner, and cleaned up the house. I never thought of drinking or doing drugs during this time. Little did I know, it comes back at an inopportune time.

I soon met a man I will call Joe. He seemed nice, so we went out on a few dates. I looked forward to having a couple of glasses of wine and hearing some good music. One night, while I was at home sitting at the kitchen table talking with Joe, my ex-boyfriend came over unexpectedly. Joe told me to let him in, and this turned out to be a huge mistake. My ex-boyfriend had a look in his eyes that seemed even more strange than I remembered. He had a gun on his belt, was carrying a knife, and he looked at me and smiled scarily.

Before I could say a word, Joe grabbed the gun and began to beat my ex in the head to the point where I thought he would kill him. I had never seen that much blood, so I jumped on top of my ex-boyfriend to cover him, and then I passed out.

When I came to, I was soaked in blood, and as I got up, I heard several gunshots. I ran out to the hallway, where I could see Joe pointing a gun outside the front door. My ex-boyfriend was running across the street as he was being shot at. I was desperately trying to grab the gun away from Joe, but it didn't seem to faze him. He even got angry that I tried to protect my ex-boyfriend from being killed. Then I heard sirens everywhere. My ex-boyfriend was alive but injured and needed to get to a hospital for all the cuts on his head. I was mopping up blood from the floor and wasn't even making a dent. I looked in the mirror and again didn't recognize myself.

There was nothing I could do as the police were downstairs at this point. I recognized a few cops from the bar where I used to work, and after they spent a couple of hours in my apartment, they let us go without charge. The next morning, the man who owned the apartment buildings came to my apartment and served me with an eviction notice. I had to be out within a week. My daughter stayed with my sister for a while, and I stayed wherever I could, hoping to find another apartment.

It didn't take long before I was back to work at the strip club, trying to save money to get another apartment. One late night after work, someone grabbed me and pulled me into their car. It was my ex-boyfriend. He had a wild look in his eyes, and he asked me if I was going to come back to him. I said, *"No, not ever."* He immediately started choking me and slamming my head at the same time. I looked into his eyes, but they didn't look like human eyes, and he was on a mission to kill me. I fought for my life, but he only seemed to choke me harder. At that point, I had not been able to catch a breath for quite a while, and then my arms just dropped to my sides. My eyes looked out the window, and I thought of my baby girl and that she would never know me. It was very dark outside, and I knew no one would be coming to help me. Then I saw a prominent, bright figure, and immediately, a sense of peace came over me. A peace I will never forget. Even though I knew I was dying, it was ok. Everything was ok. My ex-boyfriend must have seen something, too, but it terrified him, and he ran. He left me there, not knowing if I was dead or alive. It took me so long to catch my breath, and I lay there for what felt like hours. Everything was surreal.

What just happened?

The next day, I had bright purple handprints around my neck, and I could see the ridges of his fingerprints. I was unable to speak or even make a sound for about two months. After several weeks, I thought I might never be able to speak again. Then one day, I spoke. It came back suddenly, just like when it was taken away.

I remember whispering, *"I have a voice. I have a voice."* I felt so happy that day.

There was a lot of trauma in my life, and I had no idea I was carrying it everywhere I went. I would go months without smoking, drinking, or doing drugs, but then something would happen to trigger it, and I would go on a long binge, but this time it was crack. Crack was something new at the time, and so many people were smoking it. Crack houses were popping up everywhere and it seemed like it came out of nowhere. It was like an epidemic, and I was not exempt from it. If a pile of drugs were put front of me, I would be there until it was gone. A walking zombie that couldn't think of anything else but getting the next fix, while taking pain pills and drinking liquor to come down and then do it all over again. I didn't stop to eat anything and barely drank water. There were even times when I would stop for a couple of years, and then something would trigger it.

One day, I heard that my uncle Hank had gotten saved in prison, but no one really believed it, and neither did I. You had to know Hank. Ever since I was very little, I was afraid of him. He was always high, and I remember he had a cast on his foot every time I saw him. He had been in and out of prison for selling heroin and for gun charges. Hank owned an antique store in North Minneapolis and sold guns and heroin in the back room of the store. He also robbed seven

73

banks and a Brink's truck. Law enforcement couldn't seem to get him for the bank robberies, but they had enough evidence to arrest him for the Brink's truck robbery.

The FBI came looking for him one day, and he tried to run. Hank always carried two guns, and I believe he pulled one of them out, and they shot him in the chest very close to his heart. As he lay in the street, they called the coroner, but Hank wasn't dead. After being hospitalized for a while, he went to prison for quite some time, where he ran heroin through the prison. He was known to have men thrown over a balcony if they didn't pay him the money they owed him.

At that time, I was working as a dancer at an agency that sent girls to several bars in the Twin Cities. I got to know many of the dancers, and most of us shared a similar background, but we were all looking for a better life. For the most part, we just survived each day. I think many of the girls had self-hatred, just like I did, and for most of their lives, too. Some of the men that came to see us were lonely and sweet. Some were crazy and would try to harm us. There was always something happening, and it became just another day in the life. We couldn't trust many of the dancers because this was a competition. This was about money.

There were five girls in particular that I had gotten to know, some more than others. One night, I was getting ready to go on stage when the payphone in the dressing room rang. It was someone calling to tell me that a friend of mine who was also a dancer was shot in the head. She did not survive. I let out a scream I will never forget. Then I fell to the floor and sobbed my heart out. Only her, her boyfriend, her three-year-old son, and God knows what happened that night. Then, one by one, over the next couple of years, four more dancers I knew were killed at the hands of a man. I would have been the first one to die, but for some reason, I survived. I couldn't understand why I lived and they did not.

I took all kinds of street and prescription drugs. It numbed the pain for a while, but then I would come down and need more. I would do anything for drugs at that point, and it was truly a sad existence.

Many times, I would run into people I hadn't seen for a while, and it became common to hear, *"I thought you would be dead by now! I'm glad to see you are still here."*

One day, while I was living in a crack house, the others went to buy some crack, so I waited at the house. No one was there, and I wasn't high yet. I was listening to the radio, and believe me, I never did that. I was way too high to want to hear music coming out of the radio. A song came on that I remembered from years ago. It was, **Come Together** by the Youngbloods. When it got to the part where they said,

"When the one that left us here, returns for us at last", I said out loud, *"Oh Jesus, that reminds me of you."* At that very second, the dial abruptly changed on the radio, and I felt the room clear out.

I actually felt the room clear out. I said out loud, *"What just happened?"*

The very next day, I was in another room in that house, and I took one hit of crack, and immediately, I heard all of the voices around me coming into the room and telling me what they were going to do to me. There were high-pitched voices, deep and loud voices that sounded like thunder, and crazy little voices all at the same time. It felt like my eyes were glued shut, and I couldn't open them at all. I felt like my neck was being cut, and I could even feel warm blood pouring out of it. I thought my right hand had been cut off and part of my leg. I screamed and cried for what turned out to be two hours.

Then, when I thought I was going to die, I whispered the name, *"Jesus."*

Suddenly, I felt a wind come down from way above the left side of me, and then the room cleared out. I couldn't believe that the Lord Jesus would bother coming or sending an angel to come down and rescue me from the demons that were tormenting me. But he did. It took me a long time that day to be able to open my eyes and see again.

After the horrible experience, I stayed at a temporary shelter downtown for a few days. I never wanted to go back to smoking crack or living in that house again. I called my uncle Hank, who opened a Christian halfway house for women getting out of prison. I asked if I could come and stay at the halfway house, as I needed help. He said, *"You can come here, but you have to go through treatment first, and you can't tell anyone that you are my niece."*

Within two days, I was living at the halfway house, preparing to go into a six-week treatment program that was two hours away. While in treatment, I was able to deal with some things, meet people who were going through the same thing, and live far from cities.

I met a man named Jack who had come straight from prison, and we were making small talk at a table in the common area. He told me he had just gotten out of a specific prison and I responded, *"My uncle was in that prison for a long time."*

He said, *"What's your uncle's name?"* I said, *"Hank."*

He asked, *"Hank who?"* When I told him my uncle's full name, Jack had a look on his face of both seriousness and fear.

"Two pistol, Hank is your uncle?" he said.

I responded, *"That's what you call him?"*

He said, *"That's what everyone calls him."*

Then Jack went on to tell me that he once owed Hank money for heroin and couldn't pay him. Because he knew that Hank would have men thrown over balconies if they didn't pay what they owed him, Jack automatically thought it was over for him.

One day, Hank came to Jack's prison cell, and he was carrying a bible under his arm. Jack had no idea what to think, but he was afraid to turn his back as he thought Hank would kill him. Instead, Hank asked Jack to forgive him. Jack thought it was some kind of scam, but it was real. The Lord Jesus Christ had saved Hank. Jack could not understand how someone that cruel and apparently without conscience could be saved. But he was saved, and Hank went on to help people for much of his life, and I am one of those people. Hank and one of the house mothers brought me to the Lord in 1987.

I wish I could say that was the end of the hard road of stripping, prostitution, and addiction, but it wasn't. I fell backward fast when I met up with my old friends who lived in the same apartment building I moved into. I went to treatment five times, but for me, it was only a drying-out period. Sometimes it was immediate, and sometimes it took several months to stay clean. The bible says, *"As a dog returns to its vomit, so a fool repeats his folly."* (Proverbs 26:11) That was me. I overdosed many times, and one time, I woke up in the ICU, asking where I was. The nurse said, *"You are in the ICU. We didn't think you were going to make it."* THIS was how it was in my life and almost became the *"norm"*.

There came a time when I was going through a three-month withdrawal. Twenty-four hours a day during this withdrawal, I could hear demon voices. They all had different voices, some very deep, some almost sounded like a cartoon voice, some were whispers, but they all were telling me they were going to kill me.

There came a point where I was nearing the end of the withdrawal, but I didn't know that at the time. I stood up and said, *"God. I don't know who I am. Who am I? Please tell me who I am."*

Three days later, I called a department store customer service line to pay my minimum balance due.

The customer service representative was a man from India. He said, *"Ma'am, you have a question?"*

I said, *"No"* with a shaky voice as I was still suffering quite a bit.

He said, *"I mean, you had a question for God? He wants me to tell you, "You are my daughter, I love you, get up, stop crying, and move forward."*

I said, *"What did you say?"*

He said, *"You know, God? The man upstairs? He wants me to tell you, "You are my daughter, I love you, get up, stop crying, and move forward."*

I fell to the floor with emotion as this man just answered the question I asked God in my house three days ago. I ended up talking to the man from India for about an hour. The way God used him was so precious, and it was the beginning of my serious walk with the Lord. I asked the Holy Spirit if I would always be addicted, and He lovingly responded, *"It is over."* Treatment did not do it; only God could do it.

When I was 30 years old and pregnant with my youngest son, I attended business school and ended up working for the largest healthcare company in the world. Currently, I work for a cybersecurity company planning very large events. I have grown so much in the Lord, and it is an everyday walk. God wasted nothing that happened in my life and brought everything full circle for the good. In late 2023, I was praying in my room, and then I saw a vision of the man who tried to kill me in 1981. Although I had not thought of this man since 1981, I did hear that he had served nine years in prison for transporting an underage girl across the state line for the purpose of prostitution. I then heard an audible voice tell me to pray for him, so I did.

Three days later, the man sent me a message on Facebook Messenger asking me to forgive him for what he did to me. He told me he was having nightmares of killing me that wouldn't go away. I responded with three words. *"I forgive you,"* and put the phone down.

Then God took me into a deep vision and showed me that He wasn't going to let me die that day, as He had a plan for me, and that wasn't it. That he needed me to do something at this time of my life, all I could do was sit in my room for a couple of hours thinking about what I just saw.

I am very aware that I shouldn't be here. Whether it was accidental, by suicide, drug overdose, at the hands of man, or even being in the wrong place at the wrong time, I shouldn't be here. BUT GOD had another plan for me.

God speaks to me in dreams and visions, many of which are prophetic and come to pass quickly.

The Holy Spirit guides me every day of my life, and there is nothing like it.

Nothing else in this world matters except for bringing truth to people and the love of the Lord, Jesus Christ.

It continues to amaze me that a horrible life could be turned around into something extraordinary.

I was thinking recently about the talents people have. I said out loud, *"What talents do I even have? How could I be of help to anyone?"* I then heard the audible voice of the Lord say, **"You have your story."**

There is something I know for sure: when we can't count on the promises of man, we can count on the promises of God. For God cannot lie, and his promises are real. He has taken every bad thing that has ever happened to me and brought it full circle for the good. He wasted nothing and I can truly say, it was all worth it. I thank God in the mighty name of Jesus every day of my life, and I seek to help others who are going through what I went through for there is HOPE. I know, because I have been there.

For I YAHWEH, say to you who were once called 'Outcast', I will heal your wounds. **- Jeremiah 30:17**

Darcy Frederick

*D*arcy Frederick's journey is a testimony of redemption and God's grace. She grew up later surrounded by addiction and pain, found herself homeless on the streets of Minneapolis as a teenager, and fell into the sex industry at just 15 years old. She endured violence, addiction, and near-death experiences – even leaping in front of a gun to save a man's life, only for him to try to take hers. But God did not let her die.

Though she became a born-again believer in Jesus Christ, Darcy struggled before finally returning to Him with a boldness she never had before. Today, she shares her story to bring hope to those battling addiction, prostitution, and violence – and to the families who love them. "To God be the glory. My story is not about what I've been through, but about how God brought me out to reach others."

THE STORY OF

SHALYN PATRICK

Where the Wounds Still Weep, Grace Still Flows

I wasn't supposed to survive this. Not the trauma. Not the statistics. Not the silence. And certainly not the memories that came back in pieces like broken glass; sharp, unexpected, and painful to the touch. But I did survive. And even now, with wounds that sometimes still weep, I stand as proof that grace never runs dry.

My name is Shalyn, the youngest of three daughters born to Sheila Smith- a woman as complicated as she was beautiful. My mother had me at 33, and unlike my sisters, I was the one she did crack with. I was, by medical definition, a crack baby. But that label never told the whole story. It didn't tell how deeply she loved us, or how much I would come to love her, not just for who she was, but even for who she wasn't able to be.

My father was in and out of prison for most of my childhood. When he wasn't locked up, he was largely absent. So, the only examples of fatherhood I had went through the men my mother dated seriously, and those relationships —like much of our home life —were unstable. Yet through all the chaos, there was something about my mother's presence that stayed consistent: her love. And for years, I clung to that love like it was the only safe place in the storm.

But the truth is, love doesn't always protect you from pain. Love doesn't always keep you fed, or warm, or watched over. Love, when filtered through the haze of addiction, can feel like abandonment dressed up in affection.

Some memories, I didn't unlock until I became a grown woman on an intentional healing journey. I used to wonder why I remembered so little of my early years until I learned that trauma has a way of stealing memory. It locks it away in the basement of your mind, not to hurt you further, but to keep you alive. As I healed, though, those locked doors began to open. The fog started lifting, and what I found underneath wasn't pretty. It was painful. Raw. Confusing. But it was the truth.

My oldest sister left home at 16, leaving my middle sister and me, just three years older than me, to survive as best we could. My mother, in and out of jail over 20 times, would disappear for sometimes weeks. Whether she was chasing sobriety in another rehab or spiraling deeper into addiction, we were often left behind to fend for ourselves.

I was just five years old the first time I remember being left home alone. My sister was seven or eight. We became each other's parents, protectors, and survival partners. We'd dig through our refrigerator and scrape together whatever snacks we could find. Some nights, our softball coach would bring us McDonald's—a gesture of kindness that I didn't fully understand until I realized how unusual it was. Most kids got tucked in at night. We got dropped off snacks and prayed nobody broke in.

The most haunting memory of that season came on Christmas morning. I was maybe five or six. We woke up to no presents and no mom. I remember waiting —hopeful, naive —thinking maybe she was hiding somewhere, ready to surprise us. But as day turned to night, and our house stayed silent, it dawned on me: no one was coming. Christmas had come, but joy had not. And I was just a little girl, learning for the first time what it felt like to be forgotten.

We didn't grow up in church. In fact, God was a stranger to me for most of my childhood. We'd show up at someone's church every few years on Easter, but that was about it. Still, there was one thing my mom insisted on: memorizing Psalm 23. She had it hanging in a gold-framed picture in our bathroom. I didn't understand it then. It felt contradictory, confusing, even. "The Lord is my shepherd, I shall not want," we recited daily... yet we wanted for everything while she was gone. Food. Safety. Comfort. Stability. I could barely read, but I knew the words by heart. What I didn't realize was that one day those words would become my lifeline.

Back-to-school season was a village effort. Our aunts, uncles, and softball coach would chip in to get us school supplies. Our cousin would clean out her closet and give us her hand-me-downs. As a child, I remember feeling excited to receive those things, but as an adult, I recognize the heartbreak beneath it. We weren't being prepared for school. We were being rescued. Again.

The deeper I got into my healing, the more my childhood memories came rushing back like floodwaters. But they weren't just moments; they were revelations. I started to understand that my mind hadn't lied to me; it had simply protected me. I remembered the events clearly, but I hadn't let myself feel them. Until now.

One of the most traumatic events of my life happened when I was just a little girl, playing in the projects with a group of neighborhood kids. My cousin pulled up in my aunt's car, and I climbed onto the back of her trunk for fun. She didn't see me. And when she drove off, I was still holding on.

I was dragged for nearly 50 feet. I remember the screaming, the gravel scraping my skin, the panic in my chest. I held on as long as I could, afraid to let go. When I finally let go, I was ripped open and bleeding. I was terrified! Not just from the pain, but from what would happen when I got home.

My sister and I walked home in disbelief as I begged her not to tell Mama. When we got there, my mother was doing drugs in the living room with company. My pants were torn from thigh to ankle, blood dripping down my legs. I stood there, trembling, while my sister told her what had happened.

She looked at me, barely blinking, and said, "Okay. Go on to the back. I got company."

No hug.

No care.

No bandage.

Just abandonment… and silence.

I went into the back room and sobbed, not from physical pain, but from a soul-level ache. I was initially scared that I was going to be punished for playing on the car. But I remember sitting there feeling like I would have rather gotten a whooping. My sister eventually came to help patch me up. Years later, when I brought up that moment to my mom, she had no memory of it.

And yet… I still say she was the best mother I ever had.

Maybe that sounds delusional to you. But I've learned that love is complex. I don't excuse her failures. But I also don't erase her effort to love us in the only way she knew how. She was broken, bound, and addicted, but she was also mine. And I loved her unconditionally.

After high school, I began to build a different life. I became a Certified Nursing Assistant, then earned degrees in graphic design, web design, and business marketing. Eventually, I received my doctorate in Christian Leadership. Today, I'm a wife, a mother of four, a best-selling author, podcast host, pastor, and business coach. I've helped others birth purpose from pain, all while continuing to heal from mine.

But the wound that has never fully healed came in April 2021.

My husband and I had just landed in Hawaii to celebrate our fifth marriage anniversary when I got the call that would shatter me. My sister's screams on the other end of the line are forever etched into my spirit:

"Mama is dead!"

She had overdosed on fentanyl. And just like that, the fear I had carried since childhood- that one day, her addiction would kill her- became my reality.

I flew home in agony, my heart split in two. One part of me felt released- as though I had always known this day would come. But the other part was paralyzed by grief. It seemed the monster she had fought her entire life had finally won.

She was 58.

We buried her 8 days later.

And from that burial, a resurrection began.

After the homegoing service, there was a heaviness that settled over me like a fog- not just because I lost my mother, but because I also lost the hope that she might one day recover. The story I had prayed for was one where she'd get clean, go deeper in God, and speak on platforms beside me as a living testimony. I imagined us sharing stages, her telling the world how she made it out. But she didn't—at least not the way I imagined. And yet… her death gave birth to something impeccable.

It was from the ashes of that loss that I founded **Grit and Grace: The Sheila Smith Foundation**.

I knew I couldn't just cry about the pain. I had to *do* something with it. And so, in 2024, I launched the nonprofit in her name- not because she recovered, but because *I did*. Our mission is overdose prevention and recovery outreach. We don't just serve people already on the road to healing; we serve those still lost in the dark, those not quite ready to surrender, those just like my mother. We meet them in the streets, at their lowest, and offer them real-time hope.

We are one of the few recovery organizations that provide help to individuals even if they're not yet ready to commit to sobriety. Why? Because love doesn't wait for readiness. Love steps in, sits down, and says, "You're still worth saving."

That's what I wish more people had told my mom. That's what I needed to hear as a little girl. And that's what I now tell others, again and again.

Our work at Grit and Grace is hard. It's messy. It's not always celebrated. But it's worth it. And every time we reverse an overdose, or deliver Narcan, or help place someone in a treatment facility, I feel my mother's story being rewritten- not erased, but redeemed. Her life didn't get a happy ending. But her name now carries purpose. Her pain gave birth to my mission.

And that mission is personal.

Because I'm not just a nonprofit founder. I'm a survivor, NO, A THRIVER.

I'm a crack baby who grew into a woman crowned by God.

I'm the girl who once slept hungry, who now feeds others.

I'm the daughter of an addict, who now mothers with intention.

I'm the girl who almost bled out emotionally but now preaches healing.

I've learned that recovery isn't just for the addicted; it's for the affected.

It's for the children. The siblings. The spouses. The ones left behind in the wake of someone else's storm.

That's why I share my story. Not because it's tidy or tied with a bow but because it's real, and because someone, somewhere, is still standing in their version of my past, wondering if they'll ever make it out.

To them, I say this:

"He heals the brokenhearted and binds up their wounds." – Psalm 147:3 (NLT)

Your wounds may still weep, but grace still flows.

I often think about how grief reshapes you. It doesn't ask for permission. It doesn't warn you. It just enters and rearranges everything. I remember feeling lost in those first months after my mother's death; angry that she left, confused about how to move forward, and ashamed of how relieved I felt that the waiting was finally over.

Yes, I said, *relieved*. That's the complexity of grief no one talks about.

There's a strange relief that comes with the finality of a long, drawn-out war. And addiction IS a war. When it ends, you don't just cry- you exhale. And then you feel guilty for exhaling. You question your love. You question your faith. You wonder if you could've done more.

I've had to surrender those questions to God.

I've had to learn that sometimes love *isn't enough* to save someone. And that doesn't make it less love.

I've also had to forgive, not just my mother, but myself. For not doing more. For wanting to give up. For surviving when she didn't.

Recovery is a choice, but redemption is a gift.

That's what I live by now.

I've poured my pain into purpose, my trauma into transformation. And while I still have hard days, I no longer live under the weight of them. I've learned how to acknowledge and manage my emotions without being ruled by them. I've learned to honor the story without staying trapped inside it.

I've also become a safe place for others, the version of me I once needed.

Today, I stand as a wife and mother of six. My husband and I are raising not just our biological children, but adopted twins. We are building a home rooted in healing, safety, and truth. The very things I once lacked are now the things I fiercely protect.

As a pastor and leader, I speak into the lives of women who think they've gone too far, made too many mistakes, or been too broken to be used. I look them in the eyes and say, "I was there too. But grace found me."

"And after you have suffered a little while, the God of all grace... will restore, support, and strengthen you."

– 1 Peter 5:10

Let me be clear: I am not the exception. I'm the evidence.

Evidence that God can redeem even the most jagged of stories.

Evidence that trauma doesn't get the final word.

Evidence that recovery is real, even if it doesn't look like what we expected.

Some people recover *from* addiction.

Some recover *through* it.

Some, like me, recover *around* it.

But all of us have the chance to rise.

All of us can turn our sorrow into seed.

I used to wonder what kind of woman my mother would've become if healing had its complete work in her. I wonder what kind of grandmother she would've been to all my children. I imagine her holding the twins, rocking them to sleep with that same soft voice I remember from childhood- the one that could calm storms even as her own raged silently inside.

But I don't live in those what-ifs anymore.

I live in the now.

And in the *now*, I'm building a legacy out of what once buried me.

Today, I mother with fierce intention. I protect, I pray, and I pay attention because I know what it feels like to be invisible in your own home. I hug my kids tighter, not out of fear, but out of reverence for how far I've come. I raise them to know God, not through memorized scriptures on a bathroom wall, but through real relationship, trust, and truth.

I love my husband deeply; the kind of love that's rooted in covenant and covered in grace. And though our family story has its own layers, it is one soaked in healing, miracles, and faith.

I'm not a perfect mother.

I'm not a flawless woman.

But I am *intentional*.

And I am *healed enough to lead*.

And maybe that's what redemption really looks like. Not forgetting the pain, but using it to our advantage. Not waiting to be spotless, but choosing to be surrendered.

"You intended to harm me, but God intended it all for good. He brought me to this position so I could save the lives of many people."

– Genesis 50:20 (NLT)

The enemy tried to bury me beneath my beginnings.

He tried to strangle me with shame.

But God repurposed every painful detail and used it to unlock doors I never knew I had keys to.

Through the lens of ministry, I've had the honor of speaking to women who still carry the ache I once held in silence. Women who are silently mothering while grieving their own mother wounds. Women who are building empires while silently managing flashbacks. Women who look powerful on paper but are secretly still trying to forgive the version of themselves that didn't know better.

To those women, I say:

You are not disqualified.

You are not too broken.

You are not behind.

You are becoming.

If you had asked me ten years ago if I'd ever share these pieces of my life so publicly, I would've told you no. Not because I was ashamed, but because I hadn't yet realized the power of my own voice. I hadn't yet realized that the very things I wanted to forget were the very *things God wanted to use*.

So many of us were taught to hide our scars. To edit our stories. To only speak once we're fully healed. However, the truth is that there is an **anointing in your honesty**. And your story doesn't need to be wrapped in a bow to be powerful. It just needs to be *true*.

That's what this book represents.

Not a highlight reel.

Not a trophy shelf.

But a sacred record of transgression and recovery- of people who dared to live honestly, love deeply, and rise anyway.

I was a child forced to grow up too fast and remember too little.

I was a woman who buried her mother with unanswered prayers and unspoken questions.

And yet, I am still here.

Not just here… but *whole*.

Not whole because everything was fixed, but because grace filled the cracks.

Not whole because the wounds don't weep but because **grace still flows**.

And now I invite others to receive that grace.

Through **Grit and Grace**, we go into the streets, the neighborhoods, the broken systems, and we interrupt cycles with compassion.

If you're reading this and carrying your own version of my story- whether you're the addict, the child, the mother, or the mourner- I want you to hear me clearly:

You can recover.

You can heal.

You can lead.

You can live.

Don't disqualify yourself because your scars still sting. Don't wait until you feel ready to rise. You will never feel fully ready. But you *are fully chosen*.

You are not your beginnings.

You are not your bloodline.

You are not what happened to you.

You are the glory that grows from broken ground.

So, tell your story, even the messy parts.

Live your truth, even if your voice shakes.

And walk in your grace, even if the wounds still weep.

Because wherever they weep…

Grace. Still. Flows.

Dr. Shalyn Patrick

Dr. Shalyn Patrick is a powerhouse of redemption, purpose, and grace. Raised in the shadows of trauma, addiction, and abandonment, she emerged from a childhood marked by pain to become a healing force for others.

Today, she is a wife, mother, pastor, business leader, podcast host, nonprofit founder, and # 1 bestselling author whose life's work centers on restoration and empowerment. Through her ministry, marketplace influence, and community work, Dr. Shalyn helps others rewrite their stories just as hers has been rewritten.

THE STORY OF

DR. ANGELA BENNETT

Will You Let Jesus Wash Your Feet?

From the very beginning, a hatred has been waged against humanity. A poison dripping from the enemy's tongue, bent on severing intimacy with God and cutting off the destiny of His people. Satan's strategies shift with the centuries, but his intent has never changed: to wipe out those who carry the image of God. He issues **death decrees**. Some written into law and sealed by kings, others whispered in the secret places of the heart. Their purpose is always the same: to silence, to destroy, to end a generation before it can rise.

But God always answers. Every time the enemy has declared death, God has responded with something greater: the shedding of blood and the raising of a deliverer.

The first decree came not from a throne but from a serpent. In Eden's Garden, Satan did not shout or strike. He whispered: *"Did God really say…? You will not surely die. For God knows that when you eat of it (the tree of life) your eyes will be opened, and you will be like God"* (Genesis 3:1–5).

In that moment, the first pattern was set:

- Doubt God's Word.
- Doubt God's goodness.
- Doubt your own identity.

Adam and Eve believed the lie, and through one act of disobedience, sin entered the world (Romans 5:12). Before death came, shame rushed in. *"Then the eyes of both of them were opened, and they realized they were naked; so they sewed fig leaves together and made coverings for themselves"* (Genesis 3:7).

This was humanity's first attempt at self-salvation. Fig leaves to cover what could not be covered. But God Himself stepped in. *"The Lord God made garments of skin for Adam and his wife and clothed them"* (Genesis 3:21). Blood was shed to cover shame. An innocent died for the guilty. And even as judgment fell, God spoke promise: *"The seed of the woman will crush the serpent's head"* (Genesis 3:15). At humanity's lowest point, God declared a Deliverer would come.

The story repeated in Egypt. Israel multiplied under slavery, and Pharaoh grew fearful. His decree was chilling: *"Every Hebrew boy that is born you must throw into the Nile, but let every girl live"* (Exodus 1:22). Another attempt to cut off the covenant line.

But God had already raised up women who feared Him more than Pharaoh. Midwives Shiphrah and Puah defied the king's command. Jochebed hid her son, then placed him in a basket on the very waters meant to drown him. The Nile became not his grave but his salvation. Pharaoh's own daughter drew Moses from the water and raised him in the palace, financing the childhood of the one who would confront her father's throne.

And when judgment came, Israel was spared not by status or strength but by blood. Lambs slain, blood painted on doorframes, the promise of protection: *"When I see the blood, I will pass over you. No destructive plague will touch you"*

(Exodus 12:13). Again, the decree of death was overturned by blood and a deliverer.

Centuries later in Persia, Haman's hatred drove him to genocide. Because Mordecai refused to bow, Haman manipulated the king to authorize destruction: *"Destroy, kill and annihilate all the Jews, young and old, women and children, on a single day"* (Esther 3:13). But God had already positioned Esther in the palace. An orphan turned queen, she was hidden in plain sight *"for such a time as this"* (Esther 4:14). Through fasting and courage, she entered the throne room uninvited, risked her life, and pleaded for her people. The decree was overturned. Haman was hanged on the very gallows he had built for Mordecai. Once again, the enemy decreed death, and God raised a deliverer.

When Jesus was born in Bethlehem, wise men came searching for the King. Herod, paranoid and enraged, issued yet another decree: *"He gave orders to kill all the boys in Bethlehem and its vicinity who were two years old and under"* (Matthew 2:16). The echo of Pharaoh's decree resounded, destroy the sons, silence the Deliverer. But God preserved His Son. Joseph was warned in a dream: *"Get up, take the child and His mother and escape to Egypt"* (Matthew 2:13). And so the Messiah lived, and redemption's plan continued.

Finally, at Calvary, Satan thought he had won. The Messiah hung beaten and bloody. Pilate's decree above His head read: *"Jesus of Nazareth, King of the Jews"* (John 19:19). To the world, it looked like defeat. To the enemy, it looked like victory. But the Cross was not defeat, it was decree. Colossians 2:14 declares, *"He cancelled the charge of our legal indebtedness, which stood against us and condemned us; He has taken it away, nailing it to the cross."*

The bloodshed was eternal redemption. The death meant to silence became the doorway to resurrection. The shame He bore stripped shame of its power forever. From Eden to Egypt, from Persia to Bethlehem, from Calvary to today, the pattern has not changed: the enemy decrees death, but God always responds with blood and a deliverer.

Shame has always been one of the enemy's sharpest weapons. He doesn't always come with swords and spears. Sometimes he comes with whispers that cling like a cloak. Shame is different from guilt. Guilt says, *"I did wrong."* Shame says, *"I am wrong."* It seeps deep into the soul, convincing us we are permanently stained, permanently unworthy, permanently disqualified.

That was the first thing Adam and Eve felt in Eden after they listened to the serpent's lie. Their eyes were opened, and suddenly what had always been innocent now seemed unbearable. They grabbed at fig leaves, trying desperately to cover themselves, and then hid from the voice of God walking in the garden. That's what shame does. It makes us cover, it makes us hide, it convinces us that God no longer wants to see us.

I have witnessed firsthand how vicious this weapon can be, not just in my own life, but across generations. Apostle Isi Igenegba once said, *"There is a shame in this world instituted by the horns of darkness and managed by demons from hell. This shame has driven many (men &) women to give up their mantles, give up their callings, give up the authority that God put inside of them, laying down the microphone God gave them to call a generation to order."* Those words pierced me. Because that is exactly what shame does. It doesn't just silence your voice in the moment; it robs your future. It convinces prophets to stay quiet, worshippers to sit down, and daughters to live as though they were orphans. It buries gifts, masks authenticity, and drives people to build lives God never asked them to build, simply to prove they are enough.

Psalm 34:5 declares a different reality: *"Those who look to Him are radiant; their faces are never covered with shame."* That word for **"faces"** in Hebrew is *panim*, which means more than physical features. It means your countenance, your whole presence, your true personhood, the deepest essence of who you are. And the word **"radiant"** itself carries the idea of *flowing together*, as if your life and God's light move in union. Shame isolates and fragments, but His presence restores flow, connection, and wholeness. Shame tries to cover your *panim*, to bury your radiance. But Scripture promises that when you look to Him, shame is stripped away and your true identity shines again in His light.

I know this not only as a truth from Scripture, but as the story of my life.

For years, shame ruled me. It convinced me that I was beyond redemption, that my choices had already defined me, and that my destiny was permanently sealed. I had stumbled into prostitution, believing that was all I was worth. Every encounter whispered the same verdict: *"This is who you are. This is all you will ever be."* I turned to cocaine for courage, for a mask to wear before the world. But the high always dissolved into emptiness. I drank to numb betrayal, but the numbness gave way to a deeper hollow.

My marriages reflected the same broken rhythm. Betrayal. Infidelity. Abuse. Control. Each wound reinforced the same lie: *"You are unlovable. You are trapped. You are not enough."*

That is how shame works. It is not passive. It is active. It builds cycles of destruction and convinces you they are impossible to break. You think you are choosing freely, but the choices become chains. You believe you are in control, but in truth, you are bound.

Looking back, I see Satan's fingerprints. Just as Pharaoh drowned sons, Haman sought annihilation, and Herod slaughtered boys in Bethlehem, the enemy targeted me, my identity, my dignity, my destiny. He didn't need a king's signature to sign my death warrant. He only needed my agreement. And with every compromise, every self-destructive choice, I enforced his decree myself.

That is still how he works today. He doesn't always raise up kings. He hands us tools of our own destruction, and we smack ourselves with them:

- Sex outside of covenant, which chains instead of frees.
- Substances that numb but enslave.
- Relationships that wound instead of heal.
- Success that masks emptiness.

These are modern death decrees. They whisper, *"You will never change. You will never be enough. You will never be clean."* And if we believe them, we carry them out with our own hands.

I lived that way for years, until the breaking point came. I could no longer carry the shame. My soul was weary of fig leaves. My heart was tired of hiding. And at my lowest place, I encountered Jesus. Not the distant Jesus of religion, but the living Christ who stoops low. The One who touched lepers, defended adulteresses, welcomed prostitutes, and called broken women *Daughter*.

It was as if He looked into the darkest part of me and asked, *"Will you let Me wash your feet?"*

Everything in me resisted. Like Peter, I wanted to cry, *"No, Lord. Not here. Not this. It's too dirty."* But His voice was both firm and tender: *"Unless I wash you, you have no part with Me."* (John 13:8).

That was the moment everything changed. I surrendered. I let Him touch the places I thought untouchable. And when I did, He did what only He can do. He washed my shame away.

Isaiah 61:10 became more than words: *"He has clothed me with garments of salvation and arrayed me in a robe of His righteousness."* Where shame had clothed me in filth, He dressed me in salvation. Where shame said, *"You are disqualified,"* He declared, *"You are chosen."* Where shame said, *"You are worthless,"* He whispered, *"You are mine."*

The Cross is the great exchange. Jesus bore shame so I would be free of it. *"For the joy set before Him, He endured the cross, scorning its shame, and sat down at the right hand of the throne of God"* (Hebrews 12:2). That joy was me. That joy was you. He looked ahead to the sons and daughters who would be restored, radiant and unashamed, and He said it was worth it.

I do not stand today because I never stumbled. I stand because He lifted me. I am not radiant because of my own strength or righteousness. I am radiant because I looked to Him, and He tore the cloak of shame away.

The prostitute became a daughter.
The addict became free.
The rejected became chosen.
The ashamed became radiant.

And if He did it for me, He can do it for you.

There is another woman whose story mirrors this same battle with shame. Mark 5 tells us of a woman who had been bleeding for twelve years. Her pain was not only physical but spiritual, emotional, and social. According to the Law, her condition made her unclean. That meant she was cut off from worship, cut off from community, cut off from belonging.

Imagine her mornings. She would wake to the same flow of blood, the same ache in her body, the same heavy reminder that she was an outcast. For twelve long years, she carried that weight. The text tells us she had *"suffered a great deal under the care of many doctors and had spent all she had, yet instead of getting better she grew worse"* (Mark 5:26). Every attempt at healing failed. Every effort left her more empty. That is the cruelty of shame. It drains you of everything while giving nothing in return.

She lived under a death decree that told her, *"You are unclean. You are excluded. You are finished."*

But then she heard about Jesus.

Somewhere deep in her spirit, faith flickered. It may have been no more than a whisper, but it was enough to move her. She thought, *"If I just touch His clothes, I will be healed"* (Mark 5:28). She did not need Him to stop the crowd. She did not need an audience or a conversation. She needed one touch.

So, she pressed through the mass of people, weak and trembling but desperate, until she reached out her hand. Her fingers brushed the edge of His robe, the hem of His garment, and everything changed.

Immediately, her bleeding stopped. She felt in her body she was freed from her suffering. And Jesus knew. Power had gone out from Him. He turned and asked, *"Who touched Me?"* (Mark 5:30).

The disciples were confused. Everyone was pressing against Him. But Jesus recognized the difference between casual contact and desperate faith. Trembling, the woman fell before Him and told Him the truth.

And then Jesus did something stunning. He renamed her. *"Daughter, your faith has healed you (made you whole (NKJV)). Go in peace and be freed from your suffering"* (Mark 5:34).

This is the only time in Scripture that Jesus directly calls a woman "**Daughter**." And that word carries more than a sense of family. In Greek, it means *"Daughter of God. Acceptable to God. Rejoicing in His peculiar care and protection."* He wasn't only telling her she was healed and whole; He was telling her she was accepted. Belonging was restored. Identity was restored. Radiance was restored.

But the revelation goes deeper when we understand what she touched. The "**hem**" of His garment was not just fabric. In Jewish culture, the corners of the garment carried covenant meaning. God commanded Israel, *"Make tassels on the corners of your garments… You will have these tassels to look at and remember all the commands of the Lord, that you may obey them"* (Numbers 15:38–39). These tassels, called **tzitzit**, were covenant reminders. They symbolized humility, obedience, and God's authority.

To touch the hem was to reach for covenant itself.

115

My friend, Dr. Shalyn, once explained it like this: the hem is the end of one thing, but the beginning of another. The seam marks where the garment ends, but the tassels flow outward like rivers without end. They represent grace that never runs dry, covenant that never ceases, promises that always reach beyond.

So, when this woman touched the hem, she wasn't grabbing cloth. She was reaching for covenant. She was declaring, *"You are the fulfillment of the Law. In You is my healing. In You is my deliverance. In You is everything I need."*

And power flowed.

Jesus could have allowed her to slip away quietly, healed but still hidden. But He refused. He wanted her to be seen. He wanted her to hear Him speak her new name. He wanted the whole crowd to know that this woman, once defined by shame, was now defined by daughterhood.

This is His way with us, too. He doesn't just stop the bleeding in secret. He calls us out and names us beloved. He doesn't only heal our bodies; He restores our identities. He doesn't just cleanse us from sin; He clothes us in belonging.

And isn't that what shame tries hardest to steal? Our name. Our sense of belonging. Our radiance. Shame whispers, *"You are not enough. You are not accepted. You do not belong."* But one touch of Jesus restores it all.

This story is not only about her. It is about us. Many live with hidden bleeding. Wounds no one sees, sins we can not shake, pain we carry silently. We bury it under work, mask it with smiles, medicate it with addictions, drown it with distractions. But deep down, they know the flow has not stopped.

We are the woman in the crowd, whispering: *"If I can just touch Him…"*

And here is the good news: the hem is still flowing. Covenant is still alive. Grace is still reaching. The tzitzit of His mercy still trail into our brokenness.

Whatever decree has defined your life can end the moment you reach for Jesus.

Because the hem is always the end of one thing and the beginning of another. The end of shame, the beginning of radiance (flowing together). The end of rejection, the beginning of belonging. The end of sin's decree, the beginning of grace's decree.

For twelve years, this woman's life was marked by shame. But in one moment of encounter, she became radiant. And the same invitation waits for you.

The night before His crucifixion, Jesus gathered with His disciples for one last meal. The weight of what was coming hung heavy in the room. He knew His hour had come. He knew betrayal was already in motion. He knew the Cross was only hours away. And in that sacred moment, He did something none of them expected.

He rose from the table, removed His outer garment, wrapped a towel around His waist, and poured water into a basin. One by one, He began to wash His disciples' feet.

This was shocking. In their culture, washing feet was the task of the lowest servant. Roads were dusty, sandals open, and feet quickly filthy. No rabbi would do such a thing. No master would stoop this low. And yet the King of Glory knelt at their feet with water and towel.

But this was more than humility. It was prophecy in action. Feet represent journey and authority. God told Joshua, *"Every place you set your foot I have given you"* (Joshua 1:3). Paul wrote, *"How beautiful are the feet of those who bring good news"* (Romans 10:15). Our feet carry us into calling, but they also pick up the dust of compromise, failure, and shame.

Jesus was saying, *"I am willing to touch the dirtiest, most hidden parts of your journey, and I will make them clean."*

When He came to Peter, the disciple recoiled. *"Lord, are You going to wash my feet?"* Jesus replied, *"You do not realize now what I am doing, but later you will understand."* Still, Peter resisted: *"No, You shall never wash my feet."* Jesus answered with piercing words: *"Unless I wash you, you have no part with Me"* (John 13:6–8).

Peter's resistance was shame. He could not bear the thought of the Master stooping that low. And isn't that what we do? We tuck our dirtiest places under the table and say, *"Not this, Lord. You wouldn't want to touch this."*

But Jesus insists. Unless He washes us, we cannot share life with Him. Religion offers fig leaves, but Jesus offers cleansing. His basin and towel pointed to something greater, the Cross. Within hours, He would stoop lower still, bearing not just dust but the filth of the world. His blood would cleanse not just feet, but souls.

Imagine His hands wrapping around each foot, water running, towel absorbing the grime. He did not flinch. He did not recoil. He said by His actions, *"I see where you have walked. I know the dirt you have picked up. And I am not afraid to touch it. I came to cleanse it."*

This is still His invitation. Not only to believe from a distance, but to let Him wash what feels untouchable.

"Do you understand what I have done for you?" He asked them after. It was more than a lesson in servanthood. It was covenant love made visible. He was showing them, and us, that He is both Deliverer and Servant. The One who cancels decrees of death is also the One who kneels to wash away shame.

And His question still lingers over every heart: *"Will you let Me wash your feet?"*

That question was the turning point of my own life. Shame had built cycles I could not escape. Prostitution told me, *"This is all you are worth."* Cocaine promised courage but stole my peace. Alcohol numbed betrayal but deepened the hollow inside me. My marriages carried the same broken rhythm, betrayal, abuse, control, each one repeating the lie that I was unlovable, trapped, never enough.

Those were the enemy's decrees over me. Just as Pharaoh tried to drown sons, Haman sought annihilation, and Herod sought to slaughter, the enemy targeted me. He did not need Pharaoh's order or Herod's soldiers. All he needed was my agreement with his lies. And for years, I carried them out myself.

But there came a breaking point. I was too weary to carry shame any longer. And in that moment of collapse, I encountered Him, not the distant Christ of religion, but the One who stoops low. The One who looks into the places you hide and asks, *"Will you let Me wash your feet?"*

I resisted, like Peter. *"Not here, Lord. Not this."* But His voice was steady: *"Unless I wash you, you have no part with Me."* And when I surrendered, He washed me clean.

In that exchange, every decree was broken.

- Prostitution was broken, and I was named *Daughter.*
- Addiction was broken, and I was declared *Free.*
- Rejection was broken, and I was called *Chosen.*
- Shame was broken, and I was made *Radiant (we flowed together).*

This is the gospel. Not theory. Not history. Life. If He could break my cycles, He can break yours.

Precious reader, maybe you hear your story in mine. Maybe you know what it is to live under shame, to bleed in secret, to carry cycles that feel unbreakable. But hear me: every decree written against you has already been nailed to the Cross. Jesus bore it. And now He kneels before you with basin and towel, asking the same question He asked me: *"Will you let Me wash your feet?"*

Because when you do, shame loses its grip, and cycles are shattered under the weight of His love.

"Those who look to Him are radiant; their faces are never covered with shame" (Psalm 34:5). That word *panim*, face, presence, personhood, reminds us that shame tries to bury our true self. But Jesus restores it.

I am no longer the prostitute - I am His Daughter.
I am no longer the addict - I am Free.
I am no longer the rejected - I am Chosen.
I am no longer the ashamed - I am Radiant.

The same can also be true for you.

Reflection Questions

Take time to pause. Journal if you can. Allow the Holy Spirit to minister to you:

1. What **"death decrees"** have I believed about myself? (e.g., I will always be broken. I will never be enough. I can not be free.)
2. Where has shame covered me, silencing my voice and burying my true identity?
3. What "fig leaves" have I tried to use to cover myself instead of letting Jesus clothe me?
4. Am I willing to press through the crowd of fear and shame to reach for the hem of His garment?
5. Where in my journey do I need to hear Jesus' voice renaming me: Daughter. Accepted. Clean. Free.
6. What would it look like today, practically and spiritually, to let Jesus wash my feet?

Jesus, my Deliverer, I recognise the death decrees spoken over my life by the enemy, by others, and even by my own words. Today, I renounce, reject, denounce, and come out of agreement with them in Your name.

I thank You for Your blood that cancels every decree of sin, shame, and death. Just as You covered Adam and Eve, preserved Moses, raised up Esther, healed the woman with the issue of blood, and washed the disciples' feet, You are also my Deliverer.

Wash me now, Lord. Wash my feet. Wash the dirt of my journey, the shame of my past, the lies I have believed, and the fear I have carried. Strip away the fig leaves. Tear off the cloak of shame.

I receive Your decree over me today: **clean, chosen, beloved, adopted, free.** I step out of cycles of destruction and into cycles of grace. I rise in my true identity, radiant, flowing together with You, unashamed, empowered by Your Spirit to walk in covenant and destiny.

In Your precious name I pray, Jesus Christ of Nazareth, Amen, Amen, and Amen.

Prophetic Declaration

Speak this aloud every day until it becomes the truth you breathe:

"I am radiant in Christ. We flow together. Shame has no hold on me. Every death decree is broken by the blood of Jesus. I walk in my true identity, chosen, adopted, beloved, and free."

Here are a few variations you can rotate through, depending on your season:

1. *"The Cross cancels every decree of shame. I am clothed in righteousness and radiance."*
2. *"I am no longer defined by my past. I am named Daughter, accepted and rejoicing in God's peculiar care and protection."*
3. *"Every cycle of destruction is broken. I am free by the blood of Jesus."*
4. *"I walk in covenant, I live in grace, I shine with His glory."*

If you remember nothing else from this chapter, let it be this:

"The enemy decrees death, but Jesus kneels to wash your feet, and His decree over you is life, freedom, and radiance."

Dr. Angela Bennett

Dr. Angela Bennett is the catalyst and heartbeat behind Esther's House and Angie B Transformations—a global movement restoring women from the ruins of addiction, exploitation, and trauma. Once trapped in those very cycles herself, Angela now walks in fierce authority as a transformation coach, 9-time bestselling author, and international speaker. Through her Powerless to Powerful podcast, devotional workbooks, and identity-rooted programs, she equips women to break free, reclaim who they are in Christ, and fulfill their divine calling. Her message is bold and unwavering: you are not too far gone. Freedom is your portion.

THE STORY OF

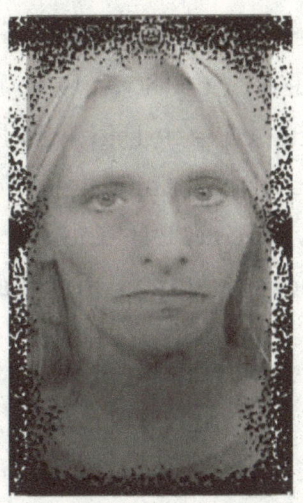

SHONNA FRYE

From Chaos to Clarity

I grew up in a small town in Indiana called Brazil. I'm the oldest of three girls, born September 28, 1970. I had what I would call a "normal" childhood. My parents were "**happily**" married, we went to church every Sunday, and neither of them smoked or drank. We went on summer vacations yearly. My parents rarely argued, and they often showed affection toward each other, as well as to my siblings and me. It felt like we were a happy family.

But when I turned 14, everything changed. My mom told my dad she had fallen out of love with him and asked for a divorce. He was crushed—and so was I. Being the oldest, I didn't understand it, and at that age, I felt like I needed my mom more than ever. She left and took my two younger sisters with her. I chose to stay with my dad.

The next few years were a blur of rebellion. I started smoking cigarettes and marijuana and ran with the wrong crowd, though I still went to school and managed decent grades. At 15, I started dating an older guy. A few years into the relationship, he became physically, emotionally, and verbally abusive—jealous fits, bruises on my arms from his grip. But I stayed, thinking it was love. It wasn't.

At 18, I got pregnant by him. I wasn't ready to raise a child, and I didn't want to have his baby. I chose to have an abortion. A couple of friends drove me to Indianapolis, and afterward, trying to numb the pain, I tried cocaine for the first time. It made me feel good. It made me forget. It helped take away the pain.

Cocaine was hard to come by in our town, but another drug soon appeared: crank—a type of speed. It was a yellowish-white substance, smelled like chemicals, and could be snorted or ingested. I split from my boyfriend and started dating one of the friends who had driven me to the clinic. The first year was a whirlwind of partying and using crank. I was in love with him.

At 22, I got pregnant again. This time felt different. I knew I wanted to keep the baby. I told the father he didn't have to stay because no matter what, I was not going to go through what I had before. He eventually changed his mind, and we decided to make it work. I quit using crank at three months pregnant and gave birth to my daughter, Haleigh, on November 22, 1993. She weighed only 5 pounds but was perfect.

Unfortunately, we resumed using crank soon after. I wanted to lose the pregnancy weight, and it worked. But when Haleigh was around two years old, we decided to quit. It wasn't fun anymore. It was expensive, and we had a child to raise. He started drinking, though I didn't see it as a problem—yet.

We bought a home, and a few months later, I found out I was pregnant again. This time, I was clean. My son, Noah, was born on September 22, 1997. I felt like I had it all—a daughter, a son, a home, a husband. We'd married in 1996. I even had my tubes tied. But he was a functioning alcoholic, and I was exhausted by the drinking and chaos. I was unhappy in my marriage and began questioning my decisions.

One day, I packed up my kids and left while he was at work. We went to a shelter in Terre Haute, and by Christmas 1999, I had a job and an apartment back in Brazil. Life was starting to stabilize. I started getting attention from and hanging out with males, mainly those much younger than I, and soon, I was introduced to meth. It was different from crank—stronger, smokable—and I quickly fell back into addiction. I even used IVs for a short period of time.

I started making many bad decisions and felt myself slipping. I was arrested for stealing some things from my husband's car, and when the police came to my house to arrest me, they found a small amount of marijuana and a muscle relaxer that I was not prescribed. I was arrested for possession of marijuana, possession of a controlled substance, and theft. While in jail for 10 days, my husband's family helped him file for divorce and custody of my children. When I was released, I had nothing. I had lost it all in 10 days! I was an absolute mess, bouncing from house to house, man to man. I would see my children when able, but was not really present.

I continued to make a series of poor choices. I missed probation appointments and violated terms. One court date, the judge gave me a choice—prison or rehab. I chose rehab and entered Richmond State Hospital. There, I learned I had hepatitis C, likely contracted from shared water used in meth injection. I was devastated.

On my 30th birthday, I left the rehab with a man much older than me. I wasn't ready for recovery. I moved back to Brazil, did house arrest, and fell deeper into addiction. Between 2000 and 2005, my life spiralled out of control. I bounced from place to place, exchanged sex for shelter, and clung to bad relationships for survival. I did things that I never thought I was capable of doing. I was pretending to be someone that I wasn't. I don't even believe that I knew who I was. I was fighting demons and keeping them very entertained. I even lived out of my car for a while. My children stayed in my life, but I felt like a shadow of myself, often contemplating ending my life.

In 2005, I tried to start fresh in Terre Haute, but I didn't change my people or things—just my location. I met a younger man and fell hard for him. He was fun, wild, and toxic. I got evicted multiple times and eventually began selling meth to survive the mess we were in—my debts, my addiction, our chaos. Soon, I was handling large quantities and earning a good income. My children were back in my life regularly, and I was going to attempt to get custody back. They were 15 and 11. But on December 11, 2008, the feds busted down my door. I had been part of a 6-month investigation, along with 18 other people. I was arrested for conspiracy to distribute methamphetamine.

That day saved my life. I remember when we drove away from my house, thinking that I was glad it was "*over*". I was oddly relieved. I had no idea where I was going or what I was facing, all I knew was that the daily "**chasing my tail**" chaos was over.

After spending some time in jail, I went to federal court and was sentenced to 72 months.

I spent a year and a half in jail before being transferred to federal prison. I flew on an airplane for the first time in my life, and it was on Con Air. I was terrified. I spent nine months at Lexington Federal Prison Camp and another year and a half in Greenville, Illinois, completing a rehab program (RDAP) that shaved a year off my sentence. The many amazing things that I learned in that program are tools that I still use to this day! I learned so much about myself, and I changed for the better. Our mantra, which we had to repeat daily, was "*change your thoughts, change your world.*" After completing the program, I got a job outside of the prison and eventually was released in September 2012 to a halfway house in Indianapolis.

While I was in prison, Haleigh was diagnosed with a rare liver disease (PSC) and gave birth to my grandson, David Damien, who had Down syndrome. He passed away at 8 months old from an infection in his heart. I'll never forget that call. I didn't know how to comfort her—I just tried to be there.

In the years that followed, I rebuilt my life and my social circle. I became a manager at Dairy Queen, waitressed at Buffalo Wild Wings and Olive Garden, and stayed clean. I became active in the recovery community. In 2021, I was accepted as a candidate in the New Citizens Program with Hamilton Center. This program is designed to assist convicted felons in their reintegration into society. I worked in four different departments during my tenure: the inpatient unit (IPU), IT, Marketing, and Access. I chose to remain in access after I successfully completed the program. This department enabled me to help those who were checking in to the facility. I took an online course while there and became a certified peer recovery coach. And because I finally had decent insurance, I was able to get treated for my Hepatitis C, and I am now cured! Soon after that, I was offered a position at a local recovery center, Wabash Valley Recovery Center, doing jail and in-office mentoring. I was also chosen to be featured on a poster for the United Way, sharing my story to give others hope.

Back in 2018, I had moved Haleigh in with me to get her stabilized. We got her benefits sorted, but her health continued to decline. She was denied a transplant three times. I was missing a lot of work to take care of her and get her to her doctor appointments.

On May 27, 2023, I was left with no choice but to call hospice. My home was a revolving door of people for the next two days.

On Monday, Memorial Day, as I was preparing to shower, I heard a voice—God's voice—telling me to go lie down with her. I held her hand, wrapped my arm around her, and told her how much I loved her. Two days later, she took her last breath with her hand in mine, lying beside me.

Nothing prepares you for that. It is truly an unexplainable loss.

I leaned on my faith and my support system to get through it.

After Haleigh passed away, I left my job at the recovery center for a role with the Vigo County Health Department as a peer recovery coach. In this position, I have flown to

California in 2024 to attend a renowned conference called AllRise, I have been trained to teach MRT, I received an award from International Overdose Awareness and Inside Out Recovery in 2023 for **"Recovery Spokesperson of the Year"**, my story and follow-ups have been featured 3 times on our local news channel, and I was nominated in 2024 by the Mental Health of America of Indiana for a Heroes

ALL RISE CONFERENCE IN ANAHEIM CALIFORNIA

for Recovery award. I now teach MRT (Moral Resonation Therapy) and Seeking Safety to inmates inside the Vigo County Jail, as well as provide peer services.

My son has blessed me with three beautiful grandchildren. He and I are very close. I've rebuilt my relationship with my parents and my sister. Sadly, in 2015, my youngest sister, Laura, passed away unexpectedly.

I've experienced unimaginable loss—but I've also found redemption. I have reestablished my relationship with God and learned a great deal about myself. I learned that it is ok to say *"no"* and to set boundaries. Recovery has given me peace, purpose, and a voice. I share my story so others know it's possible. I feel no shame for my past and my choices;

they have shaped and molded me into the woman, mother, grandmother, daughter, aunt, employee, and friend that I am today. I have been clean from meth since December 11, 2008.

One of the many things I have learned on my journey is that by the time you get clean, you will have given many people several years of proof that they should not believe in or trust you. Give it time and understand that YOU are rebuilding the damage that YOU caused.

Pray daily, keep pushing through, and persevere.

If you want it bad enough, you can get it.

And you can keep it.

Recovery is possible. A clean, healthy, fulfilling life is possible.

Shonna Frye

*S*honna Frye serves in the Social Services Division of the Vigo County Health Department in Terre Haute, Indiana. As a certified peer recovery coach, she works closely with individuals battling addiction, offering support and guidance on their recovery journeys. She also teaches Moral Reconation Therapy (MRT) and Seeking Safety programs to both male and female inmates in the Vigo County Jail, helping them build tools for transformation and healing.

Beyond her professional role, Shonna provides peer services in the community and lives out her passion for helping others in any way she can. She finds joy in spending time with her grandchildren, attending concerts, caring for her three cats, and being active in her church.

Grateful to her Lord and Savior, Jesus Christ, for the gift of life and the calling placed on her, Shonna views each day as an opportunity to serve, uplift, and share God's love with those around her.

THE STORY OF

BRONWEN HEALY

There is hope

Hope.

What is hope anyway?

We read so many quotes that encourage us to hope despite our circumstances, to believe and hope for better even when we can barely breathe, to expect and to hope for change to come even when we feel as though we are living on a cyclical hamster wheel with no perceivable way off or out; but what is hope really?

If someone were to ask you, *"What does tangible hope look like?"* what would you say, how would you respond, and could you even answer?

I believe that tangible hope is this; it is each one of us choosing to bravely sit at our computers with a blank page staring at us, calling at us to put words to the page that might somehow inspire hope, encourage hope, or to see hope bloom, perhaps even in the lives of others, and choosing just to do it. To do it because there might be somebody else's freedom on the other side of our surrendered **"yes"** to writing and sharing our own story of transgression and recovery.

Because we choose to believe that our willingness to share our own stories of hope is, in fact, a breeding ground for hope to be sown and grown into the hearts, minds, bodies, and stories of any other person who might ever come across these pages, no matter where you find yourself.

That is a beautiful definition of hope to me, and enough to give me the courage that I need to just do it…for the one.

So, here goes. May these words be tangible hope for you, just as they are for me as I type them.

The other day, as I sat in an online counselling session with one of my private practice clients, something that she said activated a response in me, and it became the polite kick up the backside that I needed to get this story written so that I could submit it before its due date. I needed the reminder that we all have times and seasons in our lives when we need hope, and that when we tell our stories of courageous overcoming, we give an invitation and an encouraging permission for others to do the same and take their own rightful place within this global hope revolution – one story at a time.

She said, *"If you can find your way out of heroin addiction and the grips of prostitution, then I do truly believe that anything is possible – that there is hope, there is always hope!"*. You see, we all have a story to tell, and this is a portion of mine.

Please consider that your friendly spoiler alert!

I recently turned 50 years old, an age that, once upon a time, I honestly never thought I would make it to. And it has got me all reflective and sentimental. When I take the time to look back over my life story, so far, some days I feel as though I have lived through enough lifetimes and survived and overcome enough stories to have a few chronicles and other days I feel as though the season that I am currently in is like the beginning of a whole new chapter and that all of this was a literal lifetime ago, which in a lot of ways, it was. So, when I considered what part of my story to tell here, let's say, I had options.

And so, it was my client's comment that sealed the fate of this story submission.

I was raised by two parents who loved me the best way that they knew how, despite their own humanity and pain; and for that, I will be forever grateful. I was born in 1975, and my dad was an alcoholic until just after my third birthday; when all our lives changed for the better, slowly but surely, as my Mum and Dad continued to fellowship with others on similar journeys. Over the years, I heard people tell their own stories of pain, transgression, recovery, and ultimately hope, and I heard my Mum tell her own story many times over, as I sat under the table in the hall while her meetings were going on. My brother is five years older than me and as we both got older, I came to a better and clearer understanding that he saw and witnessed far more trauma, anger, darkness, and chaos than my little girl eyes, heart or mind ever did. Ever aware that we were both impacted by the same family story in very different ways and that we have both carried and healed our way through those stories in our own individual ways every day ever since.

When I was 13 years old, my parents made the massive decision to move from Melbourne to Brisbane, Queensland. My older brother decided not to join us. We left him behind with the family dog, Rocky, and the only childhood home that I had ever known, and all my dear friends at the only school that I had ever attended in Moonee Ponds. The teenage years are such a crucial and pivotal time in anybody's life, and I wasn't sure how I would cope with such massive upheaval and change; time would prove that I barely did.

Like most teenagers, I had no real understanding of who I was or where I fit in, let alone how to work it all out.

I scrambled.

I tried.

I felt lonely, isolated, and sad.

I attended an elite private girls' high school in Brisbane and spent my three years there trying to fit in, all the while trying to answer those big, daunting life questions, *"Who am I?"*, *"What do I want to be when I grow up?"*, *"Where do I fit in?"*, *"Why don't I fit in?"*, *"Is there any hope in ever working it all out?"*.

I tried to hold it all together while attempting to do just that, but I never truly felt like I belonged, and after the childhood in fellowship and surrounded by treasured friends, I knew that a human's sense of belonging really mattered. That my sense of belonging really mattered.

Amid the game of trying to work out who I was and trying to fit in, I experimented with smoking cigarettes, drinking alcohol, and even tried smoking marijuana. With my family history of addiction, I understood that I could go one of two ways, really. I could not take any drugs or alcohol, or I could go all in; for most of my time in high school, I chose to barely take any, despite the regular offers from many of my friends.

I had left the private girls' school at the end of Year 10 and moved to a state high school to focus on my love of film and TV and to pursue my dreams of telling stories through that craft. I had asked my parents' permission and soon realised that permission and approval are two very different things. They had read about my new school in the newspapers and let me know that it was well known for its film, and tv, and drama departments, but it was also known for gangs and drugs.

Against their better judgment, I went anyway.

At the new school, I soon met some of the most creative and kind human beings that I had yet to know, and I was very quickly and wholeheartedly embraced by them. It no longer seemed to matter what car my parents drove, where I went for school vacations, what part of Brisbane that I lived in or how big my house was. What did matter was that I was a human with a heart and a love of creativity, film, and drama, and that was where I found my people.

And started to find, then ultimately lose, myself.

I excelled in school and flourished in the creative realm; most of my friends did too, but smoking pot and taking other drugs recreationally was also a common occurrence for them. I always said no to their offers to join them and instead chose to focus on the end game of getting the grades that I needed to get into university to study a Bachelor of Humanities, majoring in film studies. I had a dream, and I was taking the steps to make it happen. Though once I knew that I had the grades to get into my preferred course, I started to say a hearty *"yes"* to the offers to join my friends when they were smoking pot, which ended up with me being stoned most days. I then started to get curious about experimenting with other drugs; drugs that I had witnessed them consume, and they all seemed to be okay.

In those moments and throughout that season of my life, I didn't stop once to consider the generational cycles of addiction that had threatened to wipe out my family on both of my parents' sides; including the destructive and oppressive first few years of my own life due to my own

Dad's alcohol addiction issues, and how they had nearly destroyed our own family. Nor did I pause to think about how young both of my mum's parents had been when they died, heavily impacted by the ravages of alcoholism.

I was young and living in the moment, having unknowingly tricked myself into believing I was in control. Until I realised that I wasn't.

The downward spiral was a slow fade for me.

I continued to smoke pot and take other so-called **'party drugs'** on the weekends. I moved out of home and into my first of many share houses in the inner city, and the weekend drug taking soon started creeping into the other days of the week. I deferred from my dream university course at the beginning of my second year, after failing a couple of my subjects and realising that navigating the hard work required for the bachelor's degree and the seeming **'freedom and fun'** that I thought I was having in my new lifestyle no longer aligned.

I made some choices, and those choices had consequences. Please remember, I had literally grown up surrounded by other people's stories of pain and heartache and the losses associated with their loved one's addictions; and yet, here I was.

Not long after I deferred, I found out that I was pregnant. The father of the baby was my most recent boyfriend and a known heroin addict. I knew that I was in no fit state to birth a baby let alone raise a child, plus it would've stopped me from my hard partying lifestyle. I went to my doctor's office, and she encouraged me to terminate the pregnancy. She didn't even really offer any other options, and certainly, there was no talk of keeping the life inside of me alive. She made a phone call, and three days later, I had an abortion; and something inside of me died too. I had no idea of the guilt and shame that would haunt me. But it did. And all I wanted was to be numb.

That was all that I wanted.

After weeks of begging my heroin addicted boyfriend for heroin, just a little bit, despite the negative impact that I had seen the drug have on so many people that I held dear, including losing people that I cared about to overdoses, eventually, he gave in. So long as I gave him some of the drugs from what he had bought for me, he would give me some. That was his agreement. At that point, I would've done anything to be numb.

The heroin made me numb. It also made me sick.

But from that very first shot, I chose to chase the numb, in an attempt to override the sick, to try to heal the hurts; all the while, falling into a dark chasm of chaos and into a chapter of pain that I didn't think that I would ever get free from.

A numbness that I would never again be able to achieve, but a sensation that I would spend the next six years of my life chasing.

And I didn't even see or know that any of it was happening.

I was blind and I was lost; and at the age of 18, I still didn't know who I was.

Throughout those years, I did and said things that I had only ever previously seen in movies or read in books. My life felt like it was no longer my own.

The monster of heroin addiction drove me, and it was eating me alive, from the inside out. By the time I turned 21, I had spent the past few years doing my best to avoid my parents and those friends who had genuinely cared for me. I had tried to remain as functional a person as possible by holding down jobs, but only for the sake of making money to get more heroin.

I had started to become a shell of my former self.

I had been robbing things from people and selling them to the local pawn shop, and I had also been stealing from the cinema that I had worked in for years. Then one day I got caught and my boss gave me a crossroads ultimatum –I needed to decide if I was going to drug rehabilitation, or he was going to involve the police. From a place of genuine care and love, he called out my addiction, which I refused to admit to - even though I had been using heroin most days for all those years since that very first taste.

I promised him that I was going to go to a doctor to help me get into a rehab facility as soon as possible. He hugged me and let me go home…it was a day that would change my life forever.

On the bus ride home, starting to feel the internal ache in every part of my body from not having the stolen money from work to buy the heroin that I wanted to believe was going to ease the pains, I made a massive decision.

I went into the phone booth near where I was living and stole the yellow pages, then looked up **'Escort Agency'**.

I was living in a squat. I had nothing.

The only thing that I had left was my body.

I made one phone call, after the woman on the other end asked me to describe myself to her, she asked me to come and meet her for an **'interview,'** and she said, *'Come dressed ready for work tonight.'*

I had no idea what that even meant.

How does a 21-year-old, hurting, angry girl-child addicted to heroin know how to dress up, ready to sell her body to strangers, so that they can have sex with her, so that she can buy heroin?

She doesn't.

I didn't.

I was lost. Again.

I started work that night. Selling my body (and my soul) to strangers for money so that I could try to be numb. But to be able to do the work, I needed to be numb. And then I needed to take other drugs to stay awake to do the job to get the money to get the drugs, other drugs that would fool the men into thinking that I wanted to be there.

I didn't; I just wanted to be numb.

Over the next 12 months, I worked in illegal brothels, on the streets, in the daytime, through the night; all the while trying to get the fix that ever alluded me.

I was a hard worker; the fixation on wanting to be numb was the fuel that kept me showing up night after night, despite the threats, the bashings, the danger from being surrounded by the types of people who move about in the shadows.

I did things and had things done to me that no human should ever have to endure.

It was the darkest and most soul-destroying time of my life.

Then one night, I had taken heroin and speed to get ready to walk up the hill to go to work on the street corner, and there was a knock at the door. It wasn't the kind of obvious knock that sounded like the madam's dealer or the grim banging of the police; it was a gentle knock.

The next thing I heard was a voice so familiar to me that it took my breath away.

It was my Mum.

I had basically disappeared from reality and was avoiding anybody and everybody that might fully see me and genuinely care about me, even though I didn't understand that that was what I was doing at the time.

And there she was, my Mum; the person who had carried me, birthed me, raised me, protected me, and had always loved me.

Standing in the doorway of the illegal brothel where I lived and worked with my madam, who was also my heroin dealer.

With tears streaming down her face, she reached out and hugged me.

One of her infamous long lingering hugs that felt as though it had the power to wipe away all my aches and pains; all the while cracking open fresh wounds in my heart for the childhood memories that I felt like I had tarnished beyond repair, for the dreams that I felt as though I had abandoned and for the life that I truly believed that I had thrown away.

She fully saw me and truly loved me.

Her love saw past my wounds and my choices and into the truth of who I really am.

Her beloved daughter.

There is nothing like the love of a mother to draw a lost child home to her true self.

She stood there holding me close for the longest time, shaking, weeping, with arms that felt like tangible hope.

A hope that started to heal my heart from that very moment.

She reminded me that no matter where I was, or what I had been doing, or what had been done to me, there is hope.

And it brought to my remembrance a quote that I'd heard my Dad say so many times about different people in recovery in our lives, *"where there is a heartbeat, there is hope"*.

It has been a brutal but beautiful 25 or so years journey since that fateful night when my Mum found me and came to the illegal brothel, a part of the narrative story of my life that I never could've imagined, and I have a wild imagination.

Her visit, her hug, her looking me in the eye and seeing my heart and reminding me of my true identity, her passing me her phone number on a piece of paper and whispering, *"I love you, Bronwen, I am here when you are ready, there is hope"*; undoubtedly saved my life that night, literally.

I would love to say that I left the sex industry right then and there and that my life changed in that very moment. Sadly, that is not my story.

You see, the addiction and the cycle had me incredibly bound, and I didn't believe that I could get out, and to be honest, in the moment, I don't really know if I was ready to.

But a few months later, I contacted a dear old friend from high school, who also used heroin but who had always made me feel actually safe, which was very rare for me, and I asked him to help me escape the trap that I had found myself in. I knew that potentially dangerous people surrounded me and that the only option was to run away from the double life that I had created for myself. He helped me escape and let me stay with him while I detoxed the almost $1,000 a day heroin habit out of my system. To say that I thought I was going to die many times over the next ten days sounds like a grievous understatement, and even as I sit and type this out right now, my body and my heart are remembering it, all too well.

Again, I would love to say that that was it, and from that moment on, I lived free from the shackles that were holding me. Sadly, that is not my story either.

In fact, I flirted with drugs and death many more times over the next couple of years. I caused a lot of damage to myself and others, including my precious Mum, as I continued to choose the drugs, or they chose me, over anybody and anything else; winding up in more trouble, in deeper debt, and on the edge of life and sanity, more times than I can recall.

In 1999, at the age of 24, after losing two people that I held dear to heroin overdoses in a short period of time, I called my Mum's phone number and asked her for help, and told her that I really meant it that time.

Just as she had promised the night that she had come to me in the brothel, she was there for me, and I was finally ready.

She came alongside me, as only she could've, and lovingly supported me to get to a Doctor in Brisbane, who was known for helping people struggling with addiction to drugs, who believed in me and reminded her and I in my very first appointment that there was hope for me.

He had asked me about my drug history, and I had shared it with him in full detail.

He has responded with grace, kindness, and a truth that struck me —a truth that I didn't understand then, but that would soon change my life forever.

He had told me, *"Bronwen, you have a hole in your soul that only Jesus can fill"*. I had not grown up in a Christian home, but I had grown up surrounded by people from recovery fellowships, and the Serenity Prayer covered every nook and cranny of our home.

My Mum wept; she had really needed to hear that, and it became a lifeline for her and eventually for me. He had recommended a local rehabilitation support home, and I called them, and they had one spare bed coming up in two days, for a female.

Of course. The bed was for me.

It was my time.

There was hope.

That was over 26 years ago now.

A literal half a lifetime ago.

I entered that home on July 1, 1999, as an angry, lost, broken, and damaged 24-year-old girl.

In that support home, I unknowingly found grace in a thousand different ways. I had no idea that it was a Christian support home, but He did.

He had spent my entire life protecting me and saving me from myself, and now here I was - safe, with an opportunity to be healed and to begin again…again.

Through the people that worked there, the volunteers, the pastors who ran the church that it was connected to; I heard and encountered truth and a hope that literally saved me from myself and just 6 weeks into the 9 month program I surrendered my life to the loving kindness of Jesus Christ and started a transformation journey that I trust that I will be on for the rest of the days of my life.

I was fully seen, completely known, and truly loved.

That, my friends, is amazing grace.

My life now is so radically different.

I never could have imagined when I was so lost and consumed by darkness that I was created to delight, to see myself and others through eyes of hope with a heart full of grace, to look at the World with wonder and in full living colour.

I am forever growing and in the process of unbecoming and re-becoming; always on the journey of finding out who I truly am.

I am committed to healing my way to wholeness.

A choice that each one of us has, day in and day out.

Do we choose to stay stuck, or do we choose to get our hopes up?

Over the past 25+ years I have written some books, shared my story across the World, hosted outreach events for the vulnerable women that I used to be, founded and run a charity to help other women wanting life change from addictions and/or the sex industry with the core message, **"you are loved, valued and created with a purpose"**, where we had a drop in space, a social enterprise café where the women could be retrained and reskilled and reintegrated into society in a workplace where dignity and kindness flowed freely. Then, in 2019, after a car accident and what I translated to be mistreatment and unkindness from my own board, I resigned from that charity to rest, recover and heal; during which time I decided to study Counselling, where I now get the honour and privilege of coming alongside others, through private practice, and helping them to know for themselves that there IS hope; as we journey together while they process their past, learn to live well in the present and stir hope for their futures.

Every day of my life, I remember where I come from and all that I have in my life and story to be grateful for.

But never more than when I look into the eyes and see the hearts of any one of my three daughters and literally thank God for the gift that each one of them is to me. They are now all young adults living functional and free lives, walking out their own journeys of healing and restoration from the shared history that we all have together. I solo parent raised them from the ages of 2,4 and 6, a long story for another day; and every day of their lives they have seen, heard, and come to know for themselves; no matter what, despite the circumstances attached to life and the betrayal and pain that can encompass it and especially with the grief of losing my beloved Mum (their precious Nana) in 2021- that, **there IS hope.**

And in answer to my own leading question, what is hope anyway?

That is, that's it.

And to me, that is the greatest reward.

Bronwen Healy

Bronwen Healy

B ronwen Healy is an Australian-based writer, speaker, and pioneer who lives to tell of God's goodness. She has pioneered a charity in Australia that supported women wanting a life change from addictions and/or the sex industry, a thriving social enterprise, written three books, and studied to become a Counsellor to better support others to process their pasts, live in the present, and stay future-focused.

Her highest honour is being Mom to her three young adult daughters and journeying alongside them as they grow into the women that they were born to be. She is currently working on a couple of new books and has fresh dreams and hopes in her heart, **stay tuned**.

THE STORY OF

GAIL HOWELL

"Ask, and it shall be given you; seek, and ye shall find; knock, and it shall be opened unto you."
KJV Matthew 7:7

Look how far I have come

As the morning sun warms my back, I gently kneel between rows of squash, cucumbers, tomatoes, and cabbage. My fingers sink into the rich soil, teaching me how to grow what I once took for granted. I smile and breathe deeply as the breeze dances through the leaves, carrying with it the earthy scent of new life. Squirrels playfully chase each other up nearby trees, their tiny claws scratching against bark, while birds sing melodies I used to ignore.

Today I hear everything. Many years ago, I heard nothing because nothing really mattered to me. Not the garden. Not the birds. Not even my children, my family, or my friends. I had faith in God, but I was not paying attention to *Him* or *His* creations. I was not thinking about purpose, grace, or the possibility of something more. I was numb. I was lost.

Back then, ***my life was ruled by transgression***, not merely the kind I was born into, but the kind I willingly walked into. I was addicted to drugs, clinging to anything that gave me a false sense of comfort...people, places, and habits that only pulled me deeper into despair.

But God. I whisper those words as tears sting my eyes. I tilt my face toward heaven, wipe my cheeks, my heart overflowing with gratitude.

As I water my garden, I realize I have been watering my soul all along. Every leaf, every vine, every stubborn, overgrown weed reminds me both of where I came from and the life I am growing into.

This garden has become my sanctuary. It is where I reflect on *my addiction.* It is where I remember the pain of choosing *drugs versus family.* It is where I relive the uphill climb toward *sobriety*, and where I stand firmly on the foundation of **my** *faith.* Here, I offer hope *to the one still in the struggle.* Ultimately, it reminds me of the truth I live every day: *I am Sober.*

Each chapter of my story, just like every seed I have planted, has required time, patience, and the courage to dig through the dirt. By the grace of God, I am still here. *Still tending. Still healing. Still growing.*

> *"Jesus Wept."*
> *~ KJV John 11:35*

My Addiction

God heard me when I finally cried out, begging Him to take away the craving for my drug of choice. And just like that... **He did.**

During the height of my addiction, I worked at the Augusta-Richmond County Civic Center located in Augusta, Georgia. On the outside, I looked like I had it all together. I held down a job, smiled at people, and went through the motions of life as if nothing was wrong. But inside, I was crumbling.

After work, I often headed to local bars for Happy Hour, telling myself it was just to unwind, to take the edge off. It was during that season in my life that I was first introduced to marijuana, or "**weed**." It seemed harmless, social, relaxing, just something to pass the time. But it opened the door I should have never walked through.

Then came the night that changed everything. My next-door neighbor knocked on my door and casually asked, *"You wanna get high?"* Curiosity spoke louder than caution. I told myself it would be just once, just to see what it felt like. But that single decision became the doorway to my *deepest transgression.*

The first time I smoked crack cocaine, it felt like freedom, like I had finally escaped the heaviness I carried inside. But it was a lie, a trap. The more I chased it, the deeper I sank.

My focus at work slipped. My money vanished, just like my ability to parent. My smile turned into a mask I forced on each day. I barely recognized the woman staring back at me in the mirror.

My addiction didn't just destroy me. It wounded everyone who loved me. It hurt my children, my family, even my mother, whose silent worry weighed on her just as heavily as my addiction weighed on me.

But even in my chaos, God never let go. My story did not end there. The same God who watched me walk into *transgression* was already preparing the road to my *recovery*. He still had a plan for me.

Drugs versus Family

While I chased a high, I lost my family piece by piece. I lost their trust, their respect, and even their sense of safety. I loved my children, but addiction did not care about love. It did not care about responsibility. It convinced me that nothing else mattered.

During the early stages of my addiction, I was a mother raising two children, a 14-year-old daughter and a 10-year-old son. Years later, I became pregnant again. Briefly, during the pregnancy, I fought back against the pull of drugs and stayed clean. But once my son was born, I slipped right back into the same destructive habits.

It was *drugs versus family,* and drugs were winning. My addiction cost us everything. Many nights, we stayed in borrowed rooms, eating food that was not ours. Other nights, we bounced between motels, surviving wherever we could find a roof.

For more than 13 long years, drugs ruled my life. It was years of broken promises, silent tears, and crushing guilt. Then one day, I decided I was done. I no longer wanted to indulge in drugs.

I reflected on all the years of damage, on what drugs had stolen from me and my children. So, I made myself a promise: I will recover. *I will be cocaine-free.*

I knew the road ahead would not be easy. But I also knew that once I earned back my family's trust and respect, I would never again allow anyone or anything to make me lose it again.

Although the damage was done, hope was not lost. Even when love felt broken, *God was already planting the seeds of my recovery, long before I realized I was ready to grow.* That promise marked the beginning of my true recovery, one prayer, one choice, and one determined day at a time.

The Serenity Prayer
"God, grant me the serenity to accept the things
I cannot change, courage to change the things I can,
and wisdom to know the difference."
~Reinhold Niebuhr (c.1932), popularized by AA

Sobriety

The day I entered a drug-free program was the day the Serenity Prayer became my lifeline. It was then that I first learned the prayer and made the decision to become drug-free.

Before that, a woman named Samantha, a worker from the Georgia Department of Family and Children Services (DFACS), visited my residence. She was part of the Welfare-to-Work Program, designed to help DFAC recipients like me reintegrate into the workforce. But there was one requirement: I had to complete the drug-free program before being accepted into theirs.

With the Serenity Prayer as my anchor, I began turning my faith back toward God. *He* had always been present in my life, but I failed to notice. I had been ignoring *Him*, but He had not been ignoring me.

When I finally reached out, God heard my cry. My first step was to ask a friend to teach me things I didn't know about *Him*. My next step was getting baptized, an outward declaration that said, *"I am ready to change."*

I prayed. I cried. I talked to God more than I ever had before. I started over many times, beginning again and again. For a while, I did not realize God was listening, but *He* was.

Every time I whispered, *"One day at a time,"* I meant it. I had to keep repeating it until I believed it. To stay sober, I had to isolate myself, not because I did not love people, but because I did not trust myself yet, nor did I trust those around me. I had to learn to love myself again and protect my healing space.

I had to decide for myself that I wanted to live a sober life, and I did. Each sober day became a quiet victory, a seed of hope I did not even realize I was planting. God was watering every single one, slowly turning **transgression** into **recovery** and preparing me for the life I live now.

Sobriety was not just freedom from drugs; it was the first step in rebuilding everything I had lost, including my faith. As my sobriety strengthened, so did my belief that God had been guiding me all along.

My Faith

Many years later, my faith was reborn during one of the lowest points of my life. I was working at a hotel, just going through the motions, trying to hold everything together. Sometimes I made a grocery list, sometimes I didn't, but on that particular day, I did. It was just a simple list of a few things I needed to pick up after work.

The hotel where I worked had a stove and a refrigerator. That day, I was assigned to a room where a guest had purchased groceries for his extended stay. However, he had to return home unexpectedly. As I prepared to clean his room, he stopped me and said I could have the groceries he had just bought. I thanked him for his kindness, not giving it much thought about what was in the bag.

When I returned home and began unpacking the bag, I froze. One by one, I pulled out every single item that had been on my grocery list. I stared at the bag, whispered *"Wow,"* and felt tears well up in my eyes.

That moment may have seemed small to someone else, but to me, it was *everything.* It was God saying to me, *"I see you. I hear you. I will provide."* That quiet, unexpected blessing marked the beginning of my renewed faith.

From that day forward, I began to reflect on other blessings that had quietly confirmed *His* presence all along. One that stands out the most is my firstborn son, my middle child, the wild child full of energy and unpredictability. By God's grace and mercy, he has made it well past the age of 22. I knew this was no coincidence. That is faith confirmed.

My faith in my Heavenly Father is stronger than it has ever been. Not a day goes by without me thanking him for *His* mercy, *His* blessings, and *His* grace. My faith became my anchor, carrying me with hope, with courage, and with determination from transgression to recovery. Little by little, I began to see what God had been showing me all along. *He* was never absent. Every miracle, every provision, every moment of grace was *His* way of saying, *"I see you. I got you. Keep going. You are not alone. You are growing."*

To the One Still in the Struggle

If you are reading this and you are still in the middle of addiction, still hurting, still using, still wondering if you will ever feel whole again, I want you to know something: *You are not too far gone.*

It is okay to start over. It is okay to cry out to God. It is okay if all you can manage today is one small step in the right direction. You do not have to figure it all out in one day. You just have to believe that you can grow again... someday, somehow. If you ask God to help you, *He* will. But remember this: you must change your playmates and your playground if you truly want deliverance. That is what I had to do. I had to walk away from the people, places, and habits that meant me no good.

I once thought I was chasing a high, but what I was really searching for was **healing.** I wanted **peace** that did not come from a substance, **love** that did not leave, and **faith** that did not fail me.

So, *to the one still in the struggle,* hear me clearly: You are worthy of a sober life. You are worthy of rebuilding. You are worthy of grace, mercy, and second chances. Start small. Start scared. Start with one honest prayer. Then take the next step. And the next. And the next. Because even the tiniest seed can grow into something beautiful if it is planted, watered, and given light.

You may feel trapped in **transgressions** now, but recovery begins the moment you believe you deserve better. One seed of faith, one step forward, and one refusal to give up can rewrite your story. **Your garden is waiting. Plant the seed. Nurture it. Watch it grow.**

I am Sober,

My road to recovery began in September 1999. Now that *I am sober,* completely drug-free, I understand something I could not see back then: I had been chasing a feeling that was never meant to last. That first high, the euphoria, the escape, the rush, was an illusion. Yet, I spent years trying to recreate it, hoping it would numb the pain I carried from my past *transgressions.* But it never did. I never could.

171

Today, as I stand in my garden, the one I have faithfully nurtured season after season, I realize that I have been tending not just to plants, but to myself. Every seed planted, every weed pulled, every vegetable harvested has mirrored my journey from addiction to restoration. What once grew in brokenness now blooms in purpose.

This garden is no longer just soil and roots. It is my sanctuary. My redemption story. My living, breathing testimony. I am not the woman I used to be. I am still growing. I am still healing. I am still learning how to forgive myself and love myself. I am still becoming. By the grace of God... *I am sober.*

This time, I am fully present. I am awake for the miracle that is unfolding, rooted in faith, renewed in strength, and blooming with hope. I continue planting peace, purpose, and perseverance, one sacred seed at a time.

Each seed I plant is a reminder of the journey. This is not just a garden; this is my *recovery. By the grace of God... I am sober.* Here in the soil, I see how far I have come. When I pause to breathe it all in, I smile and whisper, *"Look how far I have come!"*

Gail Howell

Gail Howell, a U.S. Army Dependent, was born in Heidelberg, Germany. She was raised between Camp Gordon (also known as Fort Gordon and Fort Eisenhower), Augusta and Warrenton, Georgia. She is the mother of one adult daughter, two adult sons and 10 grandchildren.

Gail earned her Bachelor's Degree in Business Management from the University of Phoenix. If Gail isn't reading, traveling, and spending time with her children and grandchildren, she can be found tending to her garden.

A Story from One

Affected by Addiction & Trauma

Dr. Sonya Howell Barrow

BRIGHT LIGHTS, LONG SHADOWS

"I can do all things through Christ which strengtheneth me."

~ KJV Philippians 4:13

"Your tears did not weaken you; they watered the roots of who you were becoming. Your FIRE kept you alive, and your GLE showed you how to soar."
~ Dr. Sonya Howell Barrow

The lights of Times Square flashed so brightly they almost felt alive. Neon signs, digital billboards, and glowing advertisements stretched toward the night sky like stars refusing to fade. Then it appeared. The moment we had been waiting for.

Our *"Stories of"* billboard lit up in the heart of Times Square, showcasing the book covers and contributing authors from three books in the series, #1 bestsellers in multiple categories across Amazon and Barnes & Noble. I looked up, and there I was.

A photo of me was centered at the top of the first book cover display, larger than life for the world to see. These books carried not just stories, but pieces of the authors who wrote them, mine included.

I stared up at that towering screen, the warm New York air brushing against my face. Horns blared, music blasted from street performers, and people rushed by, but all I could hear was my own excited heartbeat. *This was real.*

For years, I had dreamed of moments that did not leave me feeling trapped by my past. I smiled and whispered, almost in disbelief, *"I am standing in the middle of Times Square, my success shining high above me for the world to see."*

I sent a silent prayer of thanks before turning to rejoin my youngest heartbeat, fellow authors, and our publisher. We were sharing a moment that was more than just a celebration. It was proof of how far I had come. But for me, it was not just about books or billboards. It was about survival.

As cameras flashed, I smiled for pictures, fighting back tears. Because as bright as these lights were tonight, they could not erase the long shadows of where I had come from. They could not erase the years marked by *transgression*, both mine and those I inherited, or the long road of *recovery* that brought me here.

My thoughts drifted briefly to the scared little girl who once stared into a cracked mirror, wondering who she would become. That little girl never imagined she would one day stand here, her picture shining high above Times Square.

That young girl is still inside me. But tonight, she was not scared. She felt seen. She felt redeemed. She felt celebrated.

Tonight, the world saw bestselling authors being honored in Times Square. But that young girl inside me knew the truth. This was more than a celebration. *This was recovery.*

Standing under the bright lights of New York City, I reminded myself of the same truth that carried me through every battle:

I can do all things through Christ who strengthens me. And through it all, I am still here because **I am protected in the Blood of Jesus.**

*"Even when you did not know it, your **FIRE** was already burning, **fearless** enough to survive, **inspired** enough to keep dreaming, **resilient** enough to keep going, and **empowered** enough to believe you could soar. That same **FIRE** became your **GLE**, teaching you to grow boldly, lead yourself intentionally, and elevate above your struggles endlessly."*
~ **Dr. Sonya Howell Barrow**

The Little Girl Who Had to Be Strong

Long before Times Square, before books and billboards, there was just a little girl trying to survive. From conception until now, my life has been a struggle. I was conceived by a child who had barely reached puberty. I was not planned, but I was *purposed.*

I grew up without a father or grandfather. I never experienced unconditional love from a man, nor did I have a strong male role model to teach me life lessons that guide a young girl into womanhood.

In 1986, I was 14 years old, and my mother became severely addicted to crack cocaine. Her addiction held her in its grip for 13 long years, until September 1999. During those early years, my little brothers and I were poor, sometimes hungry, and often homeless, surviving the mean streets of Augusta, Georgia.

I loved my mom deeply, even when I did not understand her. Some days she smiled at me, and I believed in her love. Other days her eyes seemed lost, as if she was trapped somewhere I could not reach. As I got older, I carried the weight of trying to hold everything together because she could not.

I was filled with questions, confusion, and silence. I learned to keep secrets, not because anyone told me to, but because even as a child, I knew some things were safer left unsaid, like how we bounced between borrowed rooms, eating food that was not ours, trying not to overstay our welcome. Or how nights in cheap motels felt like both punishment and escape, with thin sheets, strange rooms, and me pretending it was all an adventure so my brothers would not be scared.

My high school became my refuge. It was warm in the winter, cool in the summer, and free breakfast and lunch meant I had food to eat. I smiled in public, hid my pain in private, and cried silent tears into my borrowed pillow at night, carrying worries far too heavy for a teenage girl.

I became strong because I had to. Strong enough to smile in front of teachers and friends so no one would ask questions. Strong enough to help with things I did not fully understand. Strong enough to carry grown-up burdens in a young girl's body.

But that strength came with a cost.   My childhood slipped away quietly, replaced with responsibilities, fear, and a quiet promise I made to myself: **When I grow up, my life will be different. Even then, I did not realize it, but I had already begun my recovery.**

As I reflect on the woman I have become, I cannot help but smile through my tears. A *once-in-a-lifetime opportunity, I thought,* chuckling softly. But maybe not just once. There are still so many stories left for me to write.

Here I stood in the heart of Times Square, my face shining brightly above me, my youngest heartbeat at my side, my success written for the world to see. I smiled and whispered to myself, *"Look at God! Won't He do it!"*

Because long before Times Square, before books and billboards, there was just **the little girl who had to be strong.**

*"Every battle tried to break you, but your **FIRE** refused to dim. With time, your **GLE** turned that survival into strength, showing you that scars can become steppingstones."*
~ Dr. Sonya Howell Barrow

Learning Strength, the Hard Way

Strength was never given to me. It was something I had to fight for, something I had to earn the hard way. I learned it by swallowing tears I desperately wanted to let fall, by biting my tongue when every part of me wanted to scream, and by carrying responsibilities no child should have ever been expected to endure.

Whenever life felt too heavy or quitting seemed easier, I dug deep into the only strength I had, my own. I kept my head down in school, worked harder than anyone expected, stayed focused, and avoided trouble because somewhere deep down, I believed discipline was my only escape. That young girl wanted stability. She longed to be proud of herself. So, despite every obstacle, she kept going.

With time, I came to see it clearly. Every choice I made, every risk I took, every small victory was rewriting a story that once felt carved in stone. I had been born into *transgressions* that were never mine to carry but tried to claim me. But every determined step was already part of my *recovery,* long before I understood it as such.

I silenced the voices of those who mocked me, who sneered, *"Girls who live in projects are nothing but low-budget 'hoes' who will never amount to anything."* I proved them wrong. I proved it to the world. Most importantly, I proved it to that young girl inside me.

The young girl I used to be became the woman I am today. She is stronger than she ever imagined. ***"SHE IS ME."*** Long before she evolved into the woman I am now, she was already **learning strength, the hard way.**

*"Your **FIRE** made you brave enough to face what others ignored, and your **GLE** turned that courage into action… breaking chains, building legacies, and rewriting the story for those who come after you."*
~ Dr. Sonya Howell Barrow

Breaking Generational Chains

At the age of 17, during my senior year of high school, we were homeless again. I carried the weight of survival every single day, doing whatever I could just to make it through. Some nights, I stayed with my cousin. Other nights, I stayed with a young man I had been seeing, because it meant I had a roof over my head for a little while. Sometimes it did not feel like a choice, it felt like survival. But survival came with consequences, and one of those consequences would soon become my greatest blessing. I became pregnant.

In June 1990, at the age of 18 and nine months pregnant, I waddled across the stage at the Augusta-Richmond County Civic Center, graduating from T.W. Josey High School. My feet were swollen. My belly was huge. My back ached. Yet, my smile was determined. I held my head high because even then, I knew this was bigger than a diploma. This was my first act of breaking free from the transgressions I had been born into. I was already stepping into my recovery, rewriting my story one determined step at a time.

By late June 1990, I gave birth to my first heartbeat, my oldest son, Jacques. Two months later, we moved into an apartment in one of the low-income housing projects on the east side of Augusta, Georgia.

Life as a single parent was hard and the *"struggle was real."* Poverty had a way of making you feel trapped., but I refused to let it win. By the time my baby was a toddler, I enrolled at Augusta Technical Institute (now Augusta Technical College), determined to keep moving forward.

On October 15, 1992, a few months shy of my 21st birthday, I enlisted in the United States Army as a Private – E1. I did not join because it was easy. I joined because I was determined to recover, not just for myself, but for my son. I wanted more than survival. I wanted stability. I wanted my son to grow up with more than I had ever known.

The Army was not just a career choice, it was my lifeline. Every physical fitness test, every grueling road march, every training exercise that made me want to quit, I pushed through harder by thinking about my son. He was my reason. My reminder. My *"why."*

Life had already tried to break me with a mother addicted to crack cocaine, no father, homelessness, and teenage pregnancy during my high school years. Compared to that, the early days in the Army were not extremely difficult. Slowly, I felt the chains of poverty, fear, and doubt breaking, one by one. I was no longer just surviving. I was thriving and rewriting my story.

By the age of 25, I was married and living in Belgium. Because my mom was still severely addicted to crack cocaine, my husband and I adopted my 9-year-old, youngest brother and brought him to live with us. I was no longer just his older sister; I was his legal guardian. A year later I gave birth to my second heartbeat, DeShon Jr.

Life was far from perfect, but I loved deeply, protected fiercely, and kept building…not just a family, but a future. Unfortunately, even strong women face heartbreak. In 2007, after years of trying to hold a marriage together, we divorced. It was not a failure, it was a life lesson and another step in my *recovery*, choosing peace and healing over staying stuck in what no longer served me.

What started as a lifeline at the age 21 became my legacy. I went on to serve over **26 years of Active-Duty service** in the United States Army, retiring as a **highly decorated Chief Warrant Officer Five (CW5)—** Combat Veteran, achieving one of the highest and rarest ranks for an African American Female Soldier.

My *transgressions* did not define me. My *recovery* did. Every choice, every tear, every drop of blood, every ounce of sweat, every step through grit and grime was proof that I was *breaking generational chains*.

The Serenity Prayer

"God, grant me the serenity to accept the things
I cannot change, courage to change the things
I can, and wisdom to know the difference."
~Reinhold Niebuhr (c.1932), popularized by AA

The Serenity Prayer

Before I could rise, I had to surrender. I had to release the weight of years I never asked for, the *transgressions* I was born into, and the pain I carried for far too long. Choices made by others shaped my childhood and left me battling wounds I did not know how to describe.

That prayer became my anchor. It reminded me that I could not rewrite the nights spent in borrowed rooms, the confusion of loving a mother trapped in addiction, or the scars left by broken family cycles. But I could change what came next.

Each time I whispered those words, I felt strength return. The Serenity Prayer became more than a recitation; it became my lifeline. It granted me permission to stop blaming myself for what I could not control, to find courage in what I could change, and finally gain wisdom to know the difference. That clarity was the turning point of my *recovery*. It is how I stopped carrying transgressions that were not mine, and began to build the life I was meant to live.

Acceptance was only the beginning. From then on, the prayer fueled the discipline, late nights of studying while my babies slept, enduring Army training when my body begged to quit, even walking away from toxic relationships when I knew I needed a different life.

With time, wisdom followed. It helped me focus on what mattered most: my children, my faith, and my *recovery*. It reminded me to release the transgressions. It taught me to release what was beyond me and recommit to what I could change. True recovery meant letting go, and with each step, I learned how.

Little by little, survival transformed into **recovery.** Every whispered prayer and every act of intentional determination proved that I was not merely reciting *The Serenity Prayer*, I was living it.

> *"**FIRE** kept you alive when faith felt far away,*
> *and **GLE** reminded you that every hard lesson*
> *was shaping you. You did not just survive, you*
> *evolved, one determined choice at a time, into*
> *the woman you were meant to be."*
> ~ *Dr. Sonya Howell Barrow*

Looking Back

My past no longer defines me, it reminds me of how far I have come. The transgressions that once surrounded me tried to claim my future, but they did not win. What was meant to break me ignited my *FIRE*. Every obstacle became a lesson. Every struggle became proof of my determination to soar. My recovery did not happen overnight, it unfolded unapologetically, with intention. Every choice, every prayer, and every determined step moved me closer to healing.

Looking back, I know meeting my ex-husband was part of that journey, even if our marriage did not last. Recently, my oldest heartbeat asked me if I wished I had never met my ex. His question gave me pause. I had to answer honestly, both to myself and to my son. The truth? Had I not met him, my life would have taken a very different path.

When my ex and I met, I was a non-promotable Specialist – E4, counting down the days to my Expiration Term of Service (ETS). My plan was to leave the Army and return home, likely back to the same projects, the same ghetto, and the same low-income lifestyle I had fought so hard to escape. It would have been familiar. It would have been easy. But it would not have been growth. My ex strongly advised me against making that decision, especially as a single parent without a solid plan. He urged me to re-enlist, prepare for the promotion board, and secure stability before even considering leaving.

Because of his encouragement, I stayed. I re-enlisted, earned my promotable status, and advanced to Sergeant – E5, then later Staff Sergeant – E6. Even during the height of our marital struggles, he pushed me to transition from Enlisted to Warrant Officer, a decision that completely changed the trajectory of my life. If not for my ex, I would not have served over 26 years of Active-Duty service or retired as a highly decorated Chief Warrant Officer Five, one of the rarest ranks for an African American female soldier. Beyond my career, had I never met and married him, I would not have my second heartbeat, my son, DeShon Jr.

Our marriage was not perfect, and it eventually ended, but it was part of the foundation that changed my future. **I do not believe my ex truly loved me, not in the way I wanted or needed. But, in his own way, he looked out for my future. Maybe it was for me, maybe it was for our family, or maybe it was simply his sense of responsibility. I will never really know. But he kept me on a positive career path, and for that, I thank him and I can acknowledge the role he played in my life.**

My past is not a chain, it is a classroom. I was strengthened by it, and I do not dwell on it. I honor it because every hardship became a steppingstone that brought me here. God was shaping me through it all. I survived. I learned. I grew. Now I soar above it all because God ain't through with me yet. **This is my reminder, and this is my looking back.**

> *"The __No__ that could have crushed you only ignited*
> *your **FIRE**, and your **GLE** took that spark and*
> *turned it into purpose, power, and elevation."*
> ~ *Dr. Sonya Howell Barrow*

Igniting My FIRE, Encouraging My GLE

My life experiences shaped the woman I am today. I refused to let obstacles, or the negative opinions of others define me. No one else has the right to write or tell my story. I hold the pen in my hand to write my story the way that I want it to be told.

The *"No's"* I heard along the way did not break me, they built me. Every closed door, every naysayer, every challenge only fueled the **FIRE** inside me. Those *"No's"* pushed me to be *fearless* in the face of adversity. They *inspired* me to chase my purpose. They demanded that I stay *resilient* when life tried to break me. They *empowered* me to live my best and blessed life.

With maturity, came wisdom. With wisdom came clarity. I learned that success was never just surviving, it was *growth, leadership, elevation,* and creating a legacy bigger than myself. I grew boldly, even when the world expected me to stay small. I learned to lead myself first, even when no one else was there to guide me. Step by step, I elevated, turning my hard life lessons into stepping stones for others to follow.

I did not realize it then, but I was evolving into my *"next best you,"* a journey I later shared in my chapter titled *"S.O. C.A.N. Y.O.U.,"* which was featured in **"Your** NEXT *Best You"* and *"Victorious Transformation"* anthologies. That transformation was my own *victorious recovery*, a reminder that *transgressions* may try to shape you, but they do not get the final say.

This is how I turned transgression to recovery. This is how I am *Igniting My FIRE, Encouraging My GLE.*

*"Your **FIRE** brought you through the dark,*
*and your **GLE** lifted you into the light.*
Times Square is not just a destination, it is a
Reminder of how far you have climbed."
~ Dr. Sonya Howell Barrow

The Woman in the Bright Lights

As I stood in Times Square, I could not help but think about everything it took to get here…the teenage girl, the single parent, the soldier who refused to let struggle define her. Every adversity, every tear, every prayer led to this moment.

The flashing lights reflecting off the buildings felt almost surreal. The billboard showcasing the covers of three bestselling books lit up a towering digital screen, shining for the world to see. There I was, not just me, the author, not just me, the woman standing in Times Square with cameras flashing, but me, the Amazon International Bestselling Author, seven times over, across multiple categories.

If you had told that 18-year-old girl, the one who graduated high school nine months pregnant and homeless because of her mother's drug addiction, that one day her work would be celebrated in the heart of New York City's Times Square, she would have laughed through tears of disbelief.

But here I was. My youngest heartbeat stood proudly beside me; his eyes bright as he looked up at the billboard, smiling. He said, *"Mama, you are doing exactly what you are meant to be doing in your life right now, writing books."* That moment meant everything, to have at least one of my heartbeats there, sharing in a victory that belonged to us.

Sadly, my oldest heartbeat was not there, and his absence weighed heavily on my heart, even in the middle of our celebration. I am keeping the promise I made to that young girl, the promise to break free from the transgressions of drug addiction, homelessness, and poverty. I keep that promise for myself and for my children, even though the choices I made to give us a better life came at a cost.

My oldest son carries resentment and anger toward me for decisions I made that he may never fully understand, and that reality breaks my heart every single day. But I will not continue to apologize for doing what was necessary to give him and his brother stability, food, clothing, and shelter. I did the best I could with the knowledge I had, and I remain unapologetic for protecting them in the only way I knew how. My love for him is unconditional, just as fierce as the day he was born, because *without him, there would be no me.*

Though I was not loved by the first two most important men in my life, my father and grandfather, it did not break me. If anything, it fueled my recovery and made me love harder. My love for myself, my children, my family, and my friends has become my strength, my healing, and my way of breaking the cycle.

This moment, standing under the dazzling lights of Times Square, was more than just success. It was proof that transgressions do not have to define you, that recovery can rewrite your story, and that love can break even the heaviest chains. **This was more than a celebration. This was the woman in the bright lights.**

> *"The shadows of your past only*
> *made the light shine brighter. Your FIRE*
> *gave you the courage to walk through*
> *them, and your GLE taught you to stand*
> *tall in the glow of your recovery."*
> *~ Dr. Sonya Howell Barrow*

Bright Lights, Long Shadows

As my thoughts returned to the present moment and the soft melodies of festivities surrounded me, I whispered a quiet prayer of gratitude. This was more than a billboard lighting up Times Square, it was proof. Proof that no matter how broken your beginning, you can rise into your own *recovery*.

Tonight, the lights of Times Square glowed all around me. Yet the brightest light was the one God placed inside me long ago, a light that refused to dim, even when life tried to snuff it out. Beneath those dazzling city lights, I clung to two powerful truths that anchored my heart: proclamations of God's unwavering presence echoing along my path. *God ain't through with me yet.* My faith makes me unstoppable and I can boldly declare, **"SHE IS ME! I defied my life's obstacles by not becoming a statistic."** What did not kill me only made me stronger and that strength will forever remind me of these **Bright Lights, Long Shadows**.

"For He hath said, I will never leave thee, nor forsake thee."
~ KJV Hebrews 13:5

"Be strong and of good courage, fear not, nor be afraid of them: for the LORD thy God, he it is that doth go with thee; he will not fail thee, nor forsake thee."
~ KJV Deuteronomy 31:6

Dr. Sonya Howell Barrow

D r. Sonya Howell Barrow is a retired U.S. Army Combat Veteran who served honorably and distinctively for over 26+ years in various organizations and deployments before retiring as a Chief Warrant Officer Five (CW5) in November 2018. She was born at Fort Gordon (previously known as Camp Gordon, now known as Fort Eisenhower), Georgia and raised between Augusta and Warrenton, Georgia. She is a mother of two adult sons, Jacques and DeShon Jr.

Dr. Sonya received her Doctor of Humane Letters from Mainseed Christian University (MCU) and achieved the credentials of Global Fellowship in Leadership Principles. As an Information Technology and Cyber Security professional, she earned her Master's Degree in Cyber Security from the University of Maryland, University College (now known as University of Maryland Global Campus).

Since her retirement from the U.S. Army, Dr. Sonya has pursued her dream as a published author. She is an Amazon International Bestselling Author, Certified Life Coach, Founder of *AuthorpreneurSonya* , CEO and Owner of The SoJaDe Group, LLC, and SoJaDe Publishing, LLC. If Dr. Sonya isn't reading, traveling, and spending time with family and friends, she is writing and motivating others by letting them know that the *"glass is always half full, never half empty."* With her faith, strong will, and determination, she chooses to be a beacon of hope and strives to encourage others to live their best lives that are filled with confidence, self-awareness, and personal growth. Dr. Sonya provides a creative, artistic space via her social media platforms and websites to showcase her non-fiction and fiction published works spanning across four distinct genres:

1. Inspire and Motivate: **Fearless. Inspired. Resilient. Empowered. -** 🔥**FIRE.**

2. Self-Help: **Growth. Leadership. Elevation. -** 🡪 **GLE.**

3. Soldier Girl: **Military Life.**

4. Entertainment: **Tantalizing. Enchanting. Ascending. -** 🍵 **TEA.**

Igniting Your 🔥**FIRE.**
Encouraging Your 🡪**GLE.**
Savoring My 🍵 **TEA.**

"Inspiring, motivating, encouraging, and entertaining readers through captivating storytelling by telling one story at a time

THE STORY OF

ERIN SPARKS

FROM HURT, THROUGH HELL, TO HEALING

Never in a million years did I think that I would be one of the THOUSANDS that I hear talked about all on the news, different media outlets, even seeing with my very own eyes. What is that, you ask? The world pandemic of ADDICTION. I had none of the predisposing factors that most people talk about when they come into various treatment homes or hospitals for detoxing and hoping to get clean and start a brand new life. But as I've learned, addiction has no respect for person, and just as many of the men and women who have walked through it, one day, I would find myself deep in the despair of addiction. The very pits of hell, as I so vividly recall. In the turbulent grips of a disease so violent, I even recall wanting death instead of walking through this very real hell. But to my surprise, God had other plans for my life. A life that was to help others up and out of the horrendous grip of addiction, to show others that WE indeed DO RECOVER, and to give/share my very own experience, strength, and hope to many who wish the very same thing that I once did, and that is to be FREE.

My life was nothing short of good. And when I mean good, I mean I was brought up in a two-parent home, both mom and dad had good jobs, and took care of my siblings and me to the utmost of their ability. Church was not an option. We were going to be there come hell or high water, lol, let me tell you. One of my granddads was a deacon, and the other pastored a church. Grandmothers who both made and left honorable marks in our small town. Aunts and uncles who made it their business to make sure they showed us what it meant to go be great and make a stance and change in the world! All around, there was nothing that pointed to me one day traveling down a path that would soon try to destroy my very existence. And although I didn't contain what others would say was a disposing factor to addiction, there was something there beneath the surface of it all. All that good. All that was seemingly great. And it would be the very start of where the enemy of my soul would start to rear his head in my life. A very patient enemy, might I add, because my life didn't take a turn for the utmost worse until almost 20 years of my being on this earth.

As I was growing up, a lot of the way life transpired back then was that children knew that their parents loved them. We were well taken care of; anything we wanted was pretty much ours. However, the lack of emotional availability and the actual saying **"I love you"** just wasn't present. Mix that with a perfectionist mother, and we've got traction, folks. Now I can add that my brother and sister had pretty tough skin, tougher than mine, and it showed as we got older. They were more open to being who they were and not really caring what anybody thought or had to say, or even trying to fit a certain mold for anybody. Me on the other hand, ehh, not so much, and it started to show in the way I saw myself and how I saw others. Even to the point of me not really being able to be true to myself and who I really was behind the scenes. I was lying to myself and to others, as well as pretty much everybody. Now, this lack of affection, plus, might I add, really high expectations, being shown at home started to bleed into other areas of my life. And, as I stated, we knew that our parents loved us; that was undeniable. However, actually showing love and verbalizing it was not a big deal in our home, and it didn't just start then and there

199

as I got older and now realize the truth —that it came from generations past. And for me, that wasn't going to work. So, my young mind started searching and working overtime for what I felt was missing at home, but in other people. People pleasing at an all-time high. I did just about anything possible to be seen, and what I thought would make people like me and draw them to me, just like it seemed to be so easy for so many other girls my age. This charade I was living in lasted all through my childhood years until I graduated high school. So much so, that I lost myself in the high of pleasing people at home and school, and living in a world that just really wasn't ME. I conformed to who I thought people wanted me to be. Oh, what a dangerous way to live. If I could tell my younger self anything, I would tell her to know her worth and live her truth according to who God has called her to be. Anything else is a big fat lie from the father of lies and the very pits of a real hell.

This persona followed me into my young adult life, and before I knew it, in the blink of an eye, I had been married twice, with two beautiful boys from each marriage. Still living a complete lie and in a fantasy world of my own, outside the will of God for my life. I'm being tossed, it seems, in this world wind spiraling downward, don't know the first thing about myself and who I am because I've spent years continuing to live my life seemingly for everybody else instead of me and who I was called to be. I have been in two marriages now that failed and were abusive to me mentally, emotionally, and physically. I was told numerous lies by both men, which were so damaging to my core and made me feel like I just needed to give up and end my life. Not to mention, in between these marriages, because I was so broken and lost, I gave myself to numerous men as I partied and drank myself into oblivion, even some one-night stands. I had come to a point where I just didn't care. Now, I loved my boys, but I always had it in the back of my mind that they definitely deserved so much better. The enemy of my soul tried to whisper to me so many times that I just needed to end my life and that they would be better off without me. Now my parents are stepping up to the plate where I was lacking, and I truly thank God for their love and support for me and my boys through all of this chaos, confusion, and mess of a life I had found us in. I'm drinking heavily to ease the pain, and all it does is ease the pain for the night, and then by morning, I'm slapped in the face all over again of how wrecked my life is, and I feel like I have no out. You know how it feels when you're on the merry-go-round and it's spinning so fast, and you want to jump off but can't, yeah, that's how my life feels at this moment. I've heard God so many times up until this point in my life to turn it all over to Him, but in my mind, I know what I'm doing, and I'm going to keep doing things and live my way, even though clearly I have no clue what I'm doing. All I know is that I'm merely existing, but trying to be the best momma I can be to my boys and figure out this mess of a life I've created and a way out.

At this point, all I want is to numb the pain that I'm experiencing. I'm holding it all in, and no one knows the hell that I'm going through in my mind. But, in the midst of all this pain, I've finally managed to pull it all together and obtain my nursing license at the age of 27, and when I tell you that I finally feel like I've accomplished something in my life that I can be proud of, my boys, and my family. I'm finally seemingly on the way up in life because I now have the means to really take care of myself and my boys. What I didn't bank on, though, is that all my baggage is steadily following me, pressed deep down, and I didn't factor in that I have not found healing from all that has transpired in my life up until this point. I'm still just a walking ticking time bomb with pain deep at its core. No God, no therapy, I've just been winging it. I've lost so much at this point, three grandparents and a best friend that I have not come to terms with, jobs, relationships, marriages, MYSELF.. I lasted at my first job out of nursing school for about 3 years, and then the pain and all my past started to rear its ugly head. It is at this point that drinking was not sufficient for me anymore, and I needed something stronger, something harder. And let me tell you, the enemy knew exactly that, and he sent it in the form of cocaine. After I started, I knew that THIS was what I needed all along, or so I **"thought"**, because of how it made everything seemingly alright. It took every care that I had in the world away, and I was in a zone that no pain could ever touch. But this was just the gateway for what was coming…... Crack cocaine. Now, let me tell you, I had no intention of going this route; I mean, seriously, who does? I've come from this great family. Been in church my whole life, who would've thought I'd be here, and yet, here I am. And to be honest, I like it, no, I love it. I get to forget that I'm even in the world, forget what I've been through and experienced. Now, nothing can touch me or hurt me anymore. But this lifestyle was hurting me, yet not only me, but my boys, my family, threatening my career, etc. But there was no stopping me now. I've hopped in the cage with the gorilla, as we addicts understand, and he's not letting me go any time soon!

In the very first stages, I thought I was able to control myself and my appetite, but who was I kidding? You have no control over yourself when you take that first hit. And literally, that's all it takes and took for me. My boyfriend at the time was just as broken as I was, and we ended up being codependent addicts. Where you saw him, you saw me, except for work, because we got high together. It wasn't long before my addiction started catching up with me at work, and before you know it, I'm pregnant once again and now without a job. I managed to stay clean for the duration of my pregnancy, which I thank God for and resulted in a beautiful baby girl, but shortly after her birth, me and my boyfriend picked right back up where we left off—this time around even HARDER. We've upped the level of addiction to crack cocaine AND crystal meth. My whole existence is simply hollow because I've completely given in to all the pain and hurt that I've endured, and some that I even caused on my own, so that it was so easy for me to revert right back to the very thing that would try to kill me. People who don't understand addiction would ask me (now) how it was so easy leaving my kids and turning to drugs, but it is really not that simple. See, I was already broken and disgusted with myself that I believed the lies of the enemy of my soul, and that is what my mind focused on. The drugs were never the problem, but simply a temporary solution to what I thought would ease the trauma and pain I endured.

By now, meth has completely taken over, and my only focus was on getting high and numbing everything I needed to be free from it all. I couldn't function without getting high or finding a solution to get the money to get my next fix. I'm walking from store to store in our small town, coming up with any lie I could think of, so people would feel sorry for me and give me money. And because our town is so small and we were a well-known family, word had traveled so fast that I was strung out on drugs. So, most of my answers were "**no**", but there were some people who just felt sorry for me and gave me money anyway. Food and eating were not even on my radar, and that, of course, caused my once healthy-looking body to deteriorate, and I became literally skin and bones. At this point, all my boyfriend and I had to our name was a car because we lost everything else. We had no place to live. My kids were eventually taken because our next-door neighbors heard us arguing so badly one night that DHR and the police, along with my parents, came and took the children and placed them in my parents' care. That very decision right there saved my precious children because I was not fit to take care of them at the time. I eventually sold everything that I had to get enough money to buy my drugs, and the rest was packed in the car that I now lived in. I bathed very seldom because I had no home, and our local gas station became my way of brushing my teeth and taking a sink bath. I have no job now because I was not the functioning addict, but the one who wouldn't be able to hold a job because my mental health had spiraled downward so terribly low. And at this point, paranoia has set in. I'm hearing voices when no one is there, seeing shadows and thinking they're out to get me, and even became suicidal at times because I was so disgusted at how my life is being lived. My boyfriend and I are now physically fighting all the time because of the voices we both were hearing, and if you know anything about the spiritual realm, it is very real. The bible talks a lot about this very topic, and many people being healed from demons. And at this point in my life, I was in need of a savior. I needed Jesus. The demons that vied for my soul were relentless and very, very real. So much so, that I reminded myself of the man who was in the tombs cutting himself.

We are now living in our car, but staying in the woods in various places when we park, because, of course, we couldn't let people see us using drugs. And our sleep was few and far between because meth causes you to stay up and not sleep. So, we're both sleep-deprived, arguing all the time and fighting with one another, and nothing was getting better, but all hell was breaking loose in our lives. We both were spiraling, and something was going to have to give before a real hard truth happened to both of us, and that was death or jail. In one horrendous night of arguing and fighting, my boyfriend at the time had received a revelation from the Lord to get me to treatment. We could not keep on going and living like this because the inevitable was bound to happen… we were going to die. I have now tried rehab 2 times, but because the urge to use is so strong, I ended up leaving the programs and going right back out to my life in the car and using meth, and because we were so connected through trauma bonding and drugs. At this time, I'm even getting the revelation that my time is coming to an end here on this earth if I continued on this path of destruction that I've found myself in. With the strength of the Lord, I finally accept that my life has become unmanageable and that I truly need help to be free from this vicious cycle I have found myself in. That savior I referred to earlier…..I needed Him. And I needed Him BAD. I needed to be free. I needed to be revived. I needed a fresh start. I needed restoration. I needed SAVING. My whole existence had drifted into a place where I found myself at rock bottom, with nothing left but to look up, get up, and allow God to come in and perform heart surgery on me. And that is exactly what He did. But it cost me something, something that I had yet to do, and at 33 years old, I finally SURRENDERED. I surrendered my way of thinking, my way of being, and my way of doing life, my way of trying to figure everything out on my own; my whole existence was now in His hands. I gave up, but in a way that was about to give me a new life and a fresh new start.

My mind was slowly starting to be renewed with the help of God and my new living situation in rehab. I was learning how to live again, because up until this point in my life, I was totally living in survival mode, fight or flight. I've been people-pleasing my way through life, living with the wounds of my past and a lot of generational sin that has been passed down from one generation to the next. As I am finally coming to my senses just as the prodigal son did, I am gaining more and more supernatural strength to be able to say that everything that's been passed down and made its way to me stops with me. I've realized that there is deep healing that has to take place in order for my life to get on the very track that God intended for me to be on. I had to lay it all at HIS feet and let go of what I thought I needed and let the Savior rescue me. Referring back to the man in the tombs in the bible, I see myself. Alone, lost, destroying my very existence, and wasting away. That is, until Jesus stepped in after I surrendered. I was broken and had lived my life up to this point the way I thought I needed to, but it only left me and the ones who loved me in the valley. In my mind, I had done enough damage, but I'm thankful for a God Who never gives up and came in right on time and made my story HIS story full of HIS glory. He turned every mess I had ever made into a message of hope. Healed broken parts of me that I thought were too far gone ever to be revived and brought back to life. But that's just what He did. God was my rescue story. He healed my broken heart and tainted mind by the renewing of His Holy Spirit. When I gave up trying and came to the very end of myself, in stepped God.

In my surrender is where I found peace, hope, healing, and love. Everything that was lost in my life was restored, everything! From my mind, to my children/family, to jobs, to home, to car, to my once stony, callous heart. I WAS FINALLY FREE from the deafening grips of addiction. And to this day, I stand 8 years clean and serene, and able to give the next person my very real experience, strength, and hope. It was a very long uphill battle, but if I know one thing, and have learned anything, surrendering my very life is what saved my life. I couldn't, but God could. He either is or He isn't, and it was MY CHOICE to make. There was a lot of hurt that happened in my life that led to a real-life hell, but to the one who's still struggling or to the person who knows of someone struggling with addiction, healing is POSSIBLE. WE DO RECOVER. It all starts with a surrendered heart. What I took from this whole experience of addiction is that you never say never. You never truly think that you could be the one who ends up struggling with the grips of addiction. I know I never thought I would, but here I am. Thankfully, recovered and free, both my husband and I are sober and are a very active part of society, helping those who are still caught in the grips of addiction. It is our pleasure to be able to help those in need because we truly know what it looks like and is like being caught in those very grips of a real and horrendous disease. We even have our own Christian bookstore and ministry named **"No One Left Behind,"** where a lot of ministry has been and will continue to be done through, which is our pride and joy, to help those who are desperate for change, just like we were 8 years ago.

What God revealed to me is that we all will have a degree of healing we'll need in this life. We may not have caused the hurt, but the healing is our responsibility. I cannot heal for anyone else; I can only heal for myself. People may even try to project the unhealed version of themselves onto others. But it is up to that individual to seek out the healing they need to live a life free and healed, lessening the chances of getting caught up in a life that is totally out of their control, leading to an addiction of any type. When you take the time to heal, you not only free yourself, but also the others who are attached to you to some degree as well. Until true healing is sought out, there are cycles that an individual will continuously find themselves in, more so dangerous than anything else, because that is where I found myself. Cycles that not only affected me, but also my children.

How do I know this truth, because now we are able to actually talk about these cycles and the damage that it cost my children and my family. I wanted to help people all my life, but there was something always missing. That missing link? I needed to first heal. Healing and therapy have opened up my eyes to real people, really hurting. My healing, now done correctly, has made me a viable source for others who so desperately need to see what it looks like to come out on the other side and realize that it is possible. I don't at all call myself, nor my husband, **"lucky"**; I say we are BLESSED! Because the real facts are that 95% of meth users fail at getting clean and staying clean. We are part of the blessed 5% who have a story to tell: that healing and recovery are possible. And I have made it my mission to share with anyone that needs to know that WE DO RECOVER, and I'm a living, breathing witness.

Erin Sparks

Erin Sparks is a native of Fayette, Alabama, where she was born and raised. At 40 years old, she is a devoted wife to her best friend and ministry partner, Kerry Sparks. Together, they serve as Associate Ministers under the leadership of Pastor Carlos Moore. Erin is also a proud mother of a blended family of eight children and the loving owner of two fur babies, Jack and Jagger.

With a background in nursing, Erin recently stepped away from her career to fully embrace her calling into ministry. She is the owner of No One Left Behind, a business that serves the community with church essentials, home décor, Bibles, and more. In addition, she leads a girls' Bible study group called God's Girls, where she mentors young women in faith and purpose.

Erin's journey has not been without challenges. Having endured abusive marriages, low self-worth, and destructive patterns, she found true healing and identity through her relationship with God. Today, she shares her testimony of resilience and redemption as a witness to God's power to restore. Her life is a living example of hope, purpose, and the truth that true worth comes from her Heavenly Father alone.

The Story of

Tessa Williams

"Woe to those who call evil good and good evil…"
-Isaiah 5:20 (…or raise a daughter in silence, shame, and
suspicion, then wonder why she grows up wielding a whip.)

How Not to Become a Dominatrix

I wasn't born the Queen of BDSM. No one handed me a whip and said, *"Congratulations, it's a dominatrix."*

If you'd told me I'd grow up to wear latex, heels, and torture people for a living, I would've blinked in shock and gone back to my kids' Bible book.

I was raised in a Christian Brethren home, quiet, conservative, emotionally constipated. No raised hands. No joyful hymns. No sex talk. Just long skirts and memory verses.

I was born in Cape Town but raised in early '80s Perth, Western Australia, where I learned two things fast:

One: I didn't look or sound like the other kids.

Two: That made people uncomfortable.

The racism wasn't always loud or violent, but it was constant. The teasing, the whispers, the quiet reminders that I didn't belong. I was the outsider. The joke!

So, I hid in libraries. Books didn't steal your schoolbag or spit at you. They didn't call you ugly or stupid or a racial slur, they learnt from their parents. Books just sat there. Waiting. Quiet. Safe.

The first time I saw a sex Renaissance painting book, a man and a woman twisted together like a biblical warning. I stared at it like it was a horror film. Everything I knew about sex came wrapped in fire, shame, and sulfur. *"Don't do it."*

"Wait for marriage." "God is watching." Apparently, He had eyes EVERYWHERE.

And if you'd asked what I wanted to be when I grew up, it changed weekly: actress, vet, journalist, fashion designer, ballerina. Didn't matter. Someone always scoffed. *"You'll never make it." "You're not smart enough." "You're not talented enough." "You're too full of yourself." "Don't get ahead of yourself."* Eventually, I stopped dreaming out loud.

But deep down, I already knew: I wasn't going to be the girl they had planned for me. Not the obedient daughter. Not a silent wife. Not the blank canvas waiting to be painted by someone else.

Something in me had already cracked. And pain, real pain, had already moved in.

It started with a bike. Bright red. A present for my 10th birthday. My joy. Riding down the street, wind in my curls, finally free. Then... BANG.

Something hit the back of my head. Hands grabbed my hair. My face slammed into the pavement. The Panopoulos boys.

We'd been friends. Just weeks earlier, we were catching tadpoles by the river. Now, they were beating the hell out of me. Fists flying. Punches landing on my body. I screamed. Curled up. I couldn't understand what I'd done.

Their father came charging out of the house, swinging a broom, and swearing in English and Greek. *"GET OFF HER! GET IN THE HOUSE, YOU BASTARDS!"*

He was furious, not at me at them. He picked me up, wiped my face with an old hanky, and kept apologising. Then I looked up the street… and saw my own father. Watching. Blank. Unbothered. I ran to him, crying. *"They hurt me. Why did you just stand there?"*

He shrugged. *"If they hurt you badly, we'd have gone to the police."*

That was it. I snapped. I screamed. And that's when he snapped back. Shoved me. Yelled in my face: *"Shut up! Shut up! SHUT UP…you mad person!"*

That was his favourite insult. **Mad person.** Like he was branding me broken.

When Mum came home from shopping, I told her what happened. My older teenage sister, smug, the golden child with the good grades, butted in. The lies that sounded like facts always rolled off her tongue with ease. She'd gotten close to the Panopoulos boys, especially the older one, in the weeks leading up to this. Funny how they never attacked her. Just me and some of the other neighbourhood girls. But unlike me, they had siblings who defended them. Wide-eyed and serious, she said I'd called their dad a drunk. That the boys were just retaliating. *"She's so mean to those boys,"* she said, shaking her head like a disappointed teacher.

I screamed that it was a lie. My fists shook with rage. And my sister smirked. Mum believed her.

I kept screaming, trying to explain, but Mum just sighed and said, *"Well… if it is true, you shouldn't be saying things like that about adults."* And just like that, the truth didn't matter.

Pain shows up early. Betrayal cuts deepest when it comes from the ones meant to protect you. And sometimes, the people who claim to love you will stand there and watch while the world beats you bloody. But it didn't stop there.

At school, I was the failure—the stupid one. The girl in the bottom classes who still got Fs.

Until one teacher finally said, *"She can't see the blackboard. Take her to get her eyes checked."*

The optometrist confirmed it. *"This child needs glasses."*

But when we got home? My sister chimed in again. *"That's just an excuse kids at school say when they're lazy."*

And just like that, no glasses. No help. No questions. Instead, I was told maybe I had a learning disability. Maybe I had a **lazy brain.** So, I believed it. Went through school blind and humiliated, convinced I was defective.

I didn't get my first real pair of glasses until my 30s when I went to get coloured contacts. The optometrist looked at me and said, *"Your eyesight is shocking. How have you coped like this?"*

When I put on those glasses, I nearly fell over. Everything had edges. Shape. Detail. For the first time in my life, I could see. And some of the anxiety that had lived in me for decades? It started to lift. Turns out, I wasn't broken. I wasn't stupid. I just couldn't see. But by then, the damage was done. Because once that kind of story gets written into you that you're nothing, that you're too much, that you're not enough, it sticks.

Even when the lenses finally come.

Dad's Fake Funeral

Dad left during my teens. Before that, the house got tense, air thick with silence, except for the constant arguments between my parents. It felt like everyone was holding their breath, waiting for something to explode. Then one day, my mum showed up at school early to collect me. She looked upset and worn thin.

She told me Dad had left a suicide note, not to end his life, but to emotionally torch the rest of ours. In it, he blamed all three of us for how miserable his life had become.

Seriously. He even brought up something I'd said as a little kid: *"When I grow up, I'm going to kill you."* I was probably five. Angry, dramatic, and not capable of murder. But apparently, he held onto that line like it was scripture.

A few days later, the police found him all the way up in Darwin. Alive. Just… running away from his own mess.

After that, he moved to Melbourne. And that's when the whispers started. The gossiping South African church community, those aunties with their headscarves and pearls had something new to feast on.

Word got out: Dad was with another woman. And when I saw the photos, I was floored.

She was nineteen and called herself **Sparks**. A young South African girl with bleach-damaged hair dyed copper-orange, thick black roots showing, and cut-off denim shorts that left nothing to the imagination. Her butt cheeks were literally hanging out. The kind of girl Dad used to call **cheap**, **fast**, and always warned me and my sister, *"men don't respect."*

And yet, there he was. Leaving his wife. Abandoning his kids. Faking his own death. All for her. The church aunties had a field day. *"Look at Miss boude,"* said one, passing around a photo.

"Yuck," said another. *"She could at least wax that toot hair,"* they cackled, flicking through photos of the girl posing in a skimpy bikini, arms wrapped around my father like she was auditioning to be the next Mrs. Williams. They were kissing like two hormonal teenagers. Passionate. Public. Pathetic.

My mum was prettier. She had more class. But there he was Dad, knee-deep in a midlife crisis, grinning like a fool while the community giggled behind closed doors. There was nothing remotely appealing about this girl. She was young, sure. But she wasn't attractive. And she didn't last long either. She wasn't his future. She was just a rebellion in fried hair and cut-off denim shorts, proof that my dad's so-called Christian morals, like his suicide letter, were completely fake.

Enter the Bogan Prince

Shortly after Dad left, we stopped going to church and Mum transferred me to a public school. She couldn't afford the private school fees anymore, and I wasn't exactly winning any Mensa awards with my grades. So off I went to the local public school, thrown into a completely different world.

Gone were the uniforms and polished shoes. This place was straight out of a '90s music video. Grunge everything.

Flannel shirts. Ripped jeans. Doc Martens. The boys wore their hair long, the girls wore their skirts short, and everyone smoked cigarettes, joints, cloves, whatever was going.

In homeroom, I got seated next to two boys and a girl named Blake. Blake was your classic **I'm not like other girls** type. The pick-me prototype. She only hung out with boys and referred to women as **females.** Enough said. One day, she turned to me and asked, *"Do you like Anton? He's looking for a girlfriend."*

He was okay. I didn't even know him. But I said yes anyway. Why not? Who were you in the '90s high school if you didn't have a boyfriend?

Anton wasn't exactly Prince Charming, but he fit the '90s cute boy grunge aesthetic, long, greasy hair, a flannel shirt, baggy jeans, and a huge sense of entitlement. He rode a motorbike that looked like it came from Toys "R" Us. Comically small. But he rode it like it was a Harley, strutting into school every morning with his helmet tucked under his arm like he was the main character, and he smoked joints that were 90% tobacco with a whisper of weed if you were lucky. He bragged like he was some seasoned stoner, but all he ever did was give himself a coughing fit and a headache.

Then there was his family. Textbook middle-class Aussie with a splash of casual sexism. His dad and brother made jokes at the expense of his overworked mum, while she

221

bustled around doing all the **woman stuff** in silence. *"Anton just loves his lamb chops,"* she'd coo, spooning food onto his plate while he nodded and smacked his lips like a bulldog waiting to be fed. Oh, and she bought him alcohol. Underage. No shame. Just another entry in the **boys will be boys** playbook.

Our relationship? Awkward from the jump. Our first hangout ended with me trying to impress him by smoking one of his dodgy joints, then vomiting. He invited me to his senior formal dance, which felt like a huge deal at the time.

That's also when he decided to introduce me to porn. Not gently. Not curiously. Like it was homework. He put on a cheesy '80s porn called **The Brat,** a VHS tape, and stared at me the whole time like he expected me to react a certain way. I laughed at the acting. It was ridiculous. Then the sex started, and I stopped laughing. It was almost medical. Clinical. Like something people shouldn't see.

I felt sick.

He turned to me and asked anxiously, *"What part of that turned you on?"*

"None of it," I said.

"You're just not trying hard enough," he groaned.

Then came the next question: *"What's your sexual fantasy?"*

So, I told him about some romantic scene in a Victorian bed, thunderstorm outside, soft candlelight.

He cut me off. *"No, no. No,"* he snapped. *"That's not a fantasy. A fantasy is a sexual position you want to try."*

Right…

After that, kissing wasn't enough.

"I love you," he'd say. *"This is what people in love do."*

And apparently, love meant doing things you didn't want to do. Along with the constant threats of him dumping me. I eventually gave in. I got tired of arguing, the guilt trips, crying, and constant pressure.

So, we tried having sex, but my body tensed up so much it was impossible. I cried and told him to slow down, said I wasn't ready. He pulled my legs every which way, trying to recreate positions he'd seen in **The Brat**. Nothing worked. Then he got frustrated and said, *"You probably don't even have a vagina."*

I laughed. *"How do I get my period then?"*

He didn't appreciate that. *"You're gonna have to grow up sometime,"* he snapped. *"If you won't do it, someone else will."*

Later that evening, Mum showed up at his house and demanded we both come out... *right now!!!*

I froze.

Anton tried to act tough, but I saw the shake in his hands and the wobble in his voice. *"I heard you brought drugs into my house, Anton."*

He froze.

"Don't you EVER bring marijuana into my home again. I'll call the police. I don't care how old you are."

He mumbled something about it being *"mostly tobacco,"* but she wasn't having it.

Mum was furious. She told me to get in the car. NOW.

As we drove, she gripped the steering wheel like it might snap in her hands. *"Your sister's pregnant,"* she said. *"I found the test in her car, and she confessed."*

Then she exploded. *"Unmarried. Halfway through uni. Pregnant by some jackass she met at a nightclub. And now she's trying to swing it back on you, saying you're worse. Saying you're bringing boys into the house. Doing drugs."*

Mum wasn't just angry. She was shattered. Tired. Defeated. She wasn't warning me; she was trauma-dumping. Like a dam had broken, and I was the only one left to mop it up.

Later, I told Anton. I was scared. What if the same thing happened to me? *"Relax,"* he said. *"If you were pregnant, I'd see you through it."*

Like that meant anything. Like that erased the pressure that never stopped.

Clueless

Anton started pulling away after our failed attempt at sex. He didn't comfort me. Didn't ask if I was okay. Just whinged about being frustrated, demanded I finish him off in other ways, and threw out threats disguised as advice. *"If you don't do it, someone else will."*

And then *"someone else"* appeared.

Alicia

I called her that because she looked like Alicia Silverstone, long blonde hair, pouty lips, wide-eyed innocence... and also had a reputation for being fast with boys.

One day, Anton casually mentioned she'd invited him to the movies. Said she had a **spare ticket.** I told him it upset me. That it felt wrong. He rolled his eyes and told me to *"get over it."*

Said they were *"childhood best friends,"* which was hilarious, because I'd never seen her around. Not once. Not in the group. Not at school. Not after school. Not at all. I told our mutual friend Blake, the tomboy I sat next to in homeroom, and thought she'd have my back. Blake just shrugged and said, *"That's why she didn't hang out with 'females.' Too jealous. Too emotional. Waaaay too much drama"*

After our final failed attempt at sex, Anton stormed off like I'd robbed him. *"You've gotta grow up sometime,"* he snapped. *"If you're not gonna do it, someone else will. Don't you ever forget that."*

The next morning at school, he was ice cold. I tried to hold his hand in the hallway, but he pulled away like I was contagious. My stomach sank. I already knew what was coming. And then it happened, right after homeroom. Anton walked up to me with Alicia beside him. No expression. No shame. He looked me dead in the eye and said, *"It's over. I'm with Alicia now."*

I cried. I begged. Told him I'd change. Said I'd try harder. Do better. I was desperate. He just shook his head. *"Nope,"* he said flatly, eyes fixed somewhere over my shoulder.

But then...

Alicia blinked at him, confused. *"What are you talking about, Anton? You and I are just friends. I have a boyfriend, Simon. That college guy I told you about when you bought that spare ticket off me."*

Then she laughed. Loud. Like she couldn't believe what she'd just walked into. She looked at me, then back at him, and backed away like, What the hell is going on?

Anton looked stunned. And humiliated. Alicia walked off, still laughing. And I walked off too. Crying. Shattered. I should've felt like I won. Like I'd been vindicated, dumped for a girl who didn't even want him. But it didn't feel like a win. It felt like proof. Proof that I wasn't enough. I felt empty. Used. Rejected.

I had tried everything to be loved. And all he gave me in return was confirmation that he never did.

Looking back, it makes sense. Anton grew up in a house where the men sat and the women served. Where his father's voice was law and his mother's silence was expected. He learned early that girls were there to meet needs, not have any. So, when he discovered porn, it didn't feel like fantasy. It felt like confirmation.

Like everything he already believed about women had just been filmed and fast-forwarded for him. He felt entitled to me just because we were dating. Entitled to Alicia just because she had a **reputation.** Entitled to every girl's **yes,** because that's what he saw in his own home and on his VHS tapes, women existing for men's pleasure, never for their own. And I was expected to play the part.

Going to school after that was rough. I went out of my way to avoid him, ducking hallways, skipping classes, pretending to be invisible. At home, I locked myself in my room and cried. Not over love. Over the aftermath of being treated like an object. I didn't want to do the sexual things he pushed for. I wasn't ready. He didn't care. He didn't appreciate me. He didn't even see me. He just wanted someone to act out his porn-addled fantasies on. A real girl with real feelings, reduced to some disposable performance. That realisation hit like a slap. I just wanted the pain to stop.

I went to the medicine cabinet and found a bottle of pills Dad had left behind. I didn't even know what they were. I just remembered he'd used them when he hurt himself at work. They were for pain, and I was in pain. There weren't many left. I wasn't trying to die. I wasn't even thinking that far ahead. I just wanted it all to stop, for a little while. So, I took them and went to school.

By the second period, it hit me. My head spun. My stomach turned. I threw up in the toilets between classes. Mascara streaked my cheeks like melted warpaint. The school nurse found me hunched over the sink. She asked what I took. I told her. Minutes later, I was in an ambulance. At the hospital, I confessed everything.

When Mum arrived, I braced myself for shouting and sobs. Something dramatic. Something maternal. Instead, she looked… irritated. *"Stop crying,"* she snapped. *"He's trash. A dope-smoker with a ratty motorbike. Looks like he rides a toy from Kmart."* Honestly, she wasn't wrong.

Then, in true Mum fashion, she pulled out a gossip magazine and started flipping through it. Found a spread of Anna Nicole Smith marrying some half-dead billionaire. *"Look at this,"* she smirked. *"You couldn't pay me enough."*

She kept going, mocking wedding dresses, insulting celebrities, and making fun of people's perms. It was her version of comfort. Distract me with sarcasm. Point at something worse. Keep me laughing just enough to stop me from falling apart. And weirdly… I appreciated it.

When I got home from the hospital, my sister, 3 months pregnant, eyes wide and serious, pulled me aside. *"What happened?"* she asked, all hushed concern.

For a second, I thought she actually cared. Then she tilted her head and said, *"Mum told me you were laughing in the hospital like a crazy person. She said you're a Maddy."* Just like that. No warmth. No compassion. Just a dig wrapped in fake sympathy.

I went straight to Mum and asked if she really said that. She looked confused. *"What? Of course not. I'd never say that."* But my sister wouldn't drop it. Kept insisting. Kept swearing it was true. I just chalked it up to one of her signature lies, mean-spirited, unnecessary, designed to hurt. She didn't need a reason. She never did.

The doctor said I needed to talk to someone. So, I did. A psychologist. The first adult who asked the kind of questions no one else ever had. By the third session, I had a label: **depression**. It felt like a diagnosis and a life sentence. They gave me antidepressants. They didn't help much.

I still felt heavy. Still cried myself to sleep. Still believed I'd failed at something all girls were just supposed to know how to do, how to be loved without getting destroyed in the process. That school year couldn't end fast enough.

Good Enough

When Mum suggested I leave school and work full-time at the daycare she worked at, I nearly cried with relief — anything to get away from school.

Her boss, Giuseppe, was a stereotypical Italian tyrant. He barked orders, forbade us from sitting during shifts, and cared more about late fees than lost kids. Literally, he forgot to pick a few up from school once. But he always remembered to chase their parents for overdue payments.

Around this time, Mum thought modelling would be good for my self-esteem. Huge mistake. Modelling at seventeen was like throwing petrol on a fire. I was already insecure, modelling just gave professionals a reason to confirm it. Even when I booked jobs, I was told, **Too short, not thin enough, not young enough** at seventeen.

Mum and Giuseppe started getting close, so when they decided to pack up and move to Sydney to start a business together, I wasn't shocked. My sister moved out shortly after having her baby, and my grandmother moved in with me. And just like that, I was alone.

And that's when I met the most toxic boyfriend of them all. If Anton was bad, Gio was Anton turned up to eleven.

I met Gio at the modelling agency. He claimed to be the son of some millionaire tycoon. In reality, he was the receptionist, short, broke, drowning in debt, and clinging to lies like they were designer labels. He wore platform shoes, styled his hair to add height, and drew on his eyebrows like he was auditioning for a K-drama and swore he was six foot. (Maybe standing on a milk crate)

I tried breaking up with him more times than I can count. He'd cry, threaten to hurt himself, manipulate my friends and grandmother, and guilt me. He called me ugly. Fat. Washed up. Told me I was lucky anyone wanted me. I lost jobs because of him. No one wanted a twitchy, aggressive boyfriend lurking around photo shoots.

And sexually, same issue as with Anton. My body would lock up. Penetration was impossible. But this time, I was done apologising. *"If you want to screw someone else, go ahead,"* I snapped. *"Just leave me the hell alone."* Of course, he didn't.

Either he enjoyed tormenting me, or no one else wanted him. Probably both. Then , Gio had a genius idea. He was going to take me to a strip club.

I'd never been to one. I pictured what TV showed back then: sad lighting, sad girls, sad men. I told him I didn't want to go. He insisted. I think he wanted me to feel insecure. Maybe get jealous. Maybe break me down a little more.

But the second I walked into that Northbridge club, everything shifted.

The women were incredible. Tall, toned, gorgeous, glam, like real-life Barbie dolls but with more attitude. Long legs, big hair, tiny waists, perfect breasts. They looked like they'd stepped out of a Baywatch episode or a music video.

And then I saw her.

Sapphire

She was something else. Honey-blonde hair, sparkling green eyes, a body that stopped time. Confident. Playful. Commanding. She looked like a cross between Pamela Anderson and Tyra Banks, and she looked similar age to me.

I bought tipping dollars and sat as close to the stage as I could. Couldn't stop smiling. Couldn't stop telling her how beautiful she was. *"You're gorgeous too,"* she said, laughing as she took my tips. I blushed.

That's when Gio noticed I was… comfortable—having a good time. So, to make sure I wasn't, he booked a lap dance with Sapphire. She looked at him and rolled her eyes. *"Take the girlfriend too? That's so rude."*

I sat awkwardly, trapped, while Gio laid compliments to Sapphire that were meant to cut me. *"Now this is a real body,"* he said. *"Bet you wish you looked like that."*

Sapphire turned to him. *"Your girlfriend's got a gorgeous body too."*

Then she winked at me. *"So sexy."* I went red.

Then Gio reached over to **playfully** snap her G-string.

Big mistake.

Sapphire slapped him, hard. *"Touch me again and I'll get you banned for life. There's no touching in this club."*

She flagged security. They dragged him out by the collar. As I started to follow, mortified, Sapphire caught my arm. *"What are you doing with that loser?"* she asked.

I mumbled, *"He's my boyfriend."*

She made a face. *"You can do so much better than THAT. Or better yet, come work here. You wouldn't have to date losers ever again. Just drain their wallets."*

I laughed awkwardly. *"Thanks, but I'm not the type. I'm not as pretty as you. I don't even have the body for it."*

She raised a brow. *"You're good enough, honey. More than good enough."*

And just like that, something clicked. The most beautiful girl I had ever seen, with the looks and confidence I envied, told me I was good enough…..Me! It changed something in me. Not instantly. Not all at once. But it planted a seed.

On the way home, I told Gio what she said. *"Of course she said that,"* he spat. *"You look like a slut."*

That word didn't sting anymore; he'd thrown it around so many times, it was worn out. Blunt. *"I'd rather be a slut than your girlfriend,"* I said.

It took two restraining orders and moving to Sydney to finally shake him off for good. But Sapphire's voice never left me. *"You're more than good enough."*

Lipstick Lies and Lingerie Lights

Sydney was a whole new ball game. Bigger, faster, louder than Perth, and it felt like home. I felt free. Free from Gio. Free from the suffocating version of myself I'd become in Perth. Determined to start fresh.

On the way, I stopped in Melbourne to catch up with some family and friends. That night, I met a well-known musician while out clubbing. I was tired of carrying around the awkward shame of virginity, like it was some stain I needed to scrub off. I told myself I wanted it gone on my own terms.

He invited me back to his hotel. I tried cocaine for the first time, chased it with a bottle of champagne, and passed out... I woke up to him inside me.

My muscles were tense. My body wasn't ready. It hurt. Bad. There was nothing tender or mutual about it. He didn't ask. He didn't wait. He just did what he wanted.

The next morning, I told him I'd been a virgin. I don't know what I expected: shock, guilt, maybe some kind of apology. Instead, he freaked out. Demanded to know how old I was. I had to show him my ID to prove I was legal. The whole scene was ridiculous.

When I finally got to Sydney, I tried to focus on the career I came to build. Modelling gigs started rolling in, TV commercials, background roles in films, and even reality shows.

But no matter how many jobs I booked, I was still being told I wasn't enough. Not tall enough. Not thin enough. Not young enough. At barely 24, I was already being cast as the mother of four in a TV ad. It didn't exactly boost my self-esteem.

I kept thinking about Sapphire and what she'd said back in Perth, and sometimes I'd drag friends to strip clubs **for fun,** but I wasn't just there for the drinks. I'd sit and stare at the dancers, wondering what it would be like to be up there. I knew I couldn't even think about it while I was living with Mum, she'd disown me. She'd already made that clear.

Then I met Mikko.

He was unlike any man I'd met before. He was quiet, kind, a little awkward, like a Finnish Harry Potter who worked in kitchens and dabbled in film and TV. He was one of the few men who didn't seem to want to consume me.

He said stripping wasn't a big deal in his country. When I told him I wanted to try it, he supported me. He said I could do it until I was ready for a family, and then he'd support us. He even talked about taking me back to Finland with him.

Mum hated him. *"What kind of man wants his wife to be a stripper?"* she asked.

I tried to explain the cultural difference, but she didn't want to hear it. *"He's using you,"* she said.

I snapped. *"Fine, I'll call off the wedding."*

She cried. I cried.

And then I walked down the aisle and married him anyway.

We moved into our first place in the city, and I finally built up the nerve to try dancing. My first club was more of a lingerie restaurant than a strip joint, **The Enchanted Cabaret Lounge.**

I expected glamor. Maybe some sisterhood. What I got was competition, cattiness, and double standards.

The girls were older, meaner, and constantly contradicting themselves. One warned me not to hustle customers; she was literally jerking someone off under the table an hour earlier. Another snapped at me for sitting too close to a client, then left early to go home with one.

When it was my turn to go on stage, I chickened out. Told the customers, *"Please don't pick me for a lap dance."*

The boss called me over. Told me to go home and come back when I was ready. So, I did.

The next night, a dancer named Bridget offered to go on stage with me. *"Just focus on me,"* she said.

We danced together, then I danced alone. And something clicked. I can do this. And I did for a few years.

Eventually, I told Mikko I was ready to start a family. I was older now. Five years into this. It was overdue. I wasn't going to be in heels forever. That's when he changed.

Almost overnight, he went from kind and supportive to cold and withdrawn. Suddenly, everything I did was wrong. He stopped touching me. Refused to have sex. Claimed we didn't have enough money. He said I'd never make money with a pregnant belly that I'd lose my figure and never work again.

I reminded him of the plan, and he said we could start a family *"when I was ready,"* remember?

Now he was backtracking. Complaining. Avoiding. And then my passport disappeared. It was my only form of ID. I turned our place upside down, ripped apart drawers, searched every pocket, every bag. Nothing.

I asked Mikko if he'd seen it. He shrugged. *"I don't know."*

I didn't stop. I booked an appointment at the fertility clinic anyway. The day before the appointment, I came home early from work, excited to prep for this next chapter. But the second I stepped inside, something felt off.

In the sink were two wine glasses. One of them had a smear of tacky bright purple lipstick on the rim, something I'd never wear. I was a gloss girl. Always had been. Then I saw Mikko, drunk and passed out in bed. I grabbed the glass and shoved it in his face. *"What is this?"*

He blinked, disoriented.

I asked again. *"Who the fuck was in our house?"*

He looked at the lipstick, grabbed the glass, and stumbled toward the sink like washing it would somehow undo it all. After a long argument, he finally admitted it. He'd met some girl in the smoking section at the pub and brought her home. But *"nothing happened."* Sure.

We missed the fertility appointment the next morning because he stormed out, and I couldn't stop crying. Soon after, he went to Finland to visit family. I thought the break would do us good. Instead, he came back colder than ever.

Then his friend called me and dropped a bombshell. Mikko had gotten drunk one night and let something slip; he'd had a vasectomy while he was in Finland. And he was cheating on me with a girl from work. Just like that, the truth fell into place. That's when I realised he'd never planned to build a life with me.

He was using me. For the citizenship. For someone to pay half the bills. And the family we were supposed to build, the life we were supposed to create - it crumbled before it even began.

Stripping wasn't paying anymore. Clubs were shutting down left and right. The few still open were drowning in dancers. More girls than customers. More hustle than hope. Some were doing everything for fifty bucks... and I do mean everything!!! I wanted out. Badly. But I couldn't leave. I had no ID. No ID meant no new job. No government assistance. No lease. No way out. I was trapped in a life I couldn't officially exist in.

I called Mum, hoping she could help. By then, she'd moved back to South Africa, dreaming of opening an orphanage after splitting with Giuseppe. She wanted to help orphans, but her own daughter was crying on the phone, and she couldn't do a thing. Mum had lost all her money and our family home due to some dodgy investments. Later, we completely lost contact after she'd returned to Perth.

I called Dad. And my sister. She had Dad completely convinced it couldn't be done. According to her, *"once you reached a certain age, the family couldn't help anymore"*. Legal nonsense. Bureaucratic dead ends. Lies dressed as logic.

So, there I was—nearly a decade without identification. It was harder than it sounds.

And Mikko? He didn't mind. I was paying half the rent, half the bills, half the groceries, keeping his Aussie dream alive. His true colours were bleeding through. The cheating was becoming more obvious. So was the hatred between us.

If I couldn't afford half the groceries after paying my share of everything else, I didn't eat. And if I didn't eat, neither did the cat. I knew I had to get out. But until then, the cat and I were sharing cans of tuna. That's when it hit me. Not in my head, in my gut. The cold, practical part.

I should probably start escorting.

Girls at work had already jumped ship. They were making real money, not just survival crumbs. I thought maybe if I told Mikko, it would snap something in him. Wake him up. Make him care. But he just shrugged. *"You gotta do what you gotta do."*

So, I did.

I sent some photos to an escort agency. They called back almost instantly and sent me on my first job—a high-end hotel in the city. I had forty cents in my pocket, I couldn't even afford a cab.

The client was an older Indian man. I met him in the lobby, I took the envelope of cash, and snapped into show mode. This was it. I'm leaving this room a prostitute.

I went through the mechanical motions of sex. When it was over, I locked myself in the bathroom and sat in the bathtub, hollow. This is my life now. I might as well get used to it.

After the client left, I called a close male friend, Saxon, another stripper. Asked him to come over. Told him I needed to scrub the memory of the client off me. With someone familiar I was attracted to. Someone who didn't make me feel like I was dying inside.

Saxon asked why the hell I was doing this, why was I in that hotel? That situation. I told him everything. He replied, half joking, half serious, said, *"You should do porn. That'd really piss Mikko off."*

Funny. Mikko always said that was the line he wouldn't cross. Porn was too public. Too traceable. His friends and his family know exactly how he was surviving in Australia. I paused. *"Not a bad idea,"* I said.

And that's how the seed was planted. When I got home, I threw my half of the rent and grocery bills on Mikko's lap and went straight to bed. No words. No fight. Just silence, thick with resentment.

Finally Gone

"Leave," I screamed. *"Just fucking leave."*

It was after Mikko smashed my favourite coffee cup, the one Mum bought me years ago, before she left for South Africa. Now it lay shattered across the floor, like everything else he touched.

"We hate each other," I said, deadpan. *"I don't love you. I don't even like you as a person."*

But Mikko wasn't going anywhere. Not while half the bills were getting paid. He started doing things just to mess with me, coming home loud, stumbling into bed, and knocking the cat onto the floor. He knew I was a light sleeper. If I woke up, it took me hours to get back to sleep.

So, I moved to the couch. He still made noise on purpose. Sleep-deprived and strung out, I was done.

Around that time, I met a male sex worker through Instagram who'd done a couple of porn scenes. I told him I was interested in shooting something **just for laughs**. He connected me with a company he'd worked for. We set a date.

Making porn was nothing like I imagined. It was boring. Awkward camera angles. Scripted sex. Physically painful and ridiculous. I had to stretch before and after, like some twisted dance class. And the acting? My acting made **"The Brat"** look Oscar-worthy.

My co-star was dressed as a vampire. In broad daylight. In a brightly lit Meriton hotel suite. He walked into the room with a fake menacing glare while I sat on the edge of the bed in lingerie. I turned to him, took one look at the ridiculous scene, and burst out laughing.

"Cut!" the director shouted. *"Everyone reset. Contessa, focus."*

I tried. I really did. But the absurdity of it all had me giggling like an idiot. They fixed my makeup, redid my hair, and we started again.

I didn't exactly keep it quiet, either. I posted behind-the-scenes clips on social media, teased the release date. I wanted Mikko to find out. Oh… And he did, thanks to his sister, who had made a full-time hobby out of stalking my socials.

For once, her gossip finally paid off. He stormed into the bedroom, red-faced and ready to explode. *"You're a fucking porn star now?"* he yelled, using my stage name like a weapon. *"Contessa Doll?"*

"Yes," I said, turning to him calmly. *"You want an autograph?"*

Red-faced and shaking, he said, *"You did things with that porn guy you never did with me."*

I giggled at the memory. *"Yeah. I did."*

Then came his big, dramatic reveal: *"You wanna know how long I've been cheating on you? Ten years."*

I blinked. *"Cool. I don't care."*

And that's when he hit me with the best news I'd heard in a decade. *"I'm moving out."*

I sat up. *"Wait, seriously?"*

When he nodded, I jumped out of bed and cheered. I danced around the room like I'd just won the lottery. He stormed out, furious.

And that's what it finally took to get the freeloading, lying, cheating, 50/50-splitting, gaslighting ex-husband out of my life.

But, as much as I loved Mikko being gone, as hard as I tried to fool myself, I couldn't handle escorting. Sure, I was buying whatever my cat and I wanted, paying rent in advance, walking out of hotel rooms with thick stacks of cash, but I felt sick. Every time!

I went to the doctor for my monthly blood test. Told him everything. Poured it all out, hoping he'd magically fix it. Maybe help me figure out how to get my ID back so I wouldn't have to keep selling my body.

Instead, he recommended antidepressants. I told him I'd tried them before and they hadn't done a thing. He suggested Zoloft. Said it had a higher success rate than most. He also told me to see a psychologist, of course.

No one, naturally, had a solution for the ID problem. So, I had to accept it: this might be forever—time to get comfortable in the discomfort.

The thing with medication. It starts small, then it creeps up. First, the anxiety came back. So, the doctor upped my Zoloft dose. Then came the side effects. I couldn't sleep. His solution? Natural sleep aids. Melatonin. Herbal teas. Lavender oil. Cute.

So, I went doctor shopping. Got a prescription for Valium. Then Xanax. And now, finally, I was in my bubble.

Comfortable. Numb. But I started gaining weight. So, I got a script for Duromine to keep it off.

It became a ritual. Wake up, take a high dose of Zoloft. Pop a Duromine before leaving the house. Then at night, depending on how wired or wrecked I felt, it was either an Xanax or a Valium. Or both. Valium was my favorite. I could take one mid-day and float through the rest like nothing mattered.

I prided myself on not being like the other escorts, the ones who needed coke or booze or who knew what to work. Not me. I'd quit drinking years earlier when I met Mikko— never touched party drugs. Never smoked weed. I told myself prescription drugs didn't count. They were medicine.

And that's how I built my comfortable little world. My carefully medicated persona. Just me and my **dolls**.

The Birth of Contessa Doll Queen of BDSM

The truth is, Contessa Doll, Queen of BDSM, wasn't born overnight. She didn't rise from the smoke, draped in leather, whip in hand. She was born quietly. On a couch. In the dark. While watching a B-grade horror movie: **Waxwork** (1988).

There he was, the Marquis de Sade, swinging a whip, quoting lines that danced somewhere between menace and poetry: *"Sex without pain is like food without taste."*

I paused the DVD. Sat in silence. That line echoed. It didn't repulse me. It stirred something.

This wasn't the grotesque, raving de Sade from the history books. This one was composed. Elegant. Dark. A portrait of power wrapped in leather, chiseled features, and long black hair. I didn't know why it stuck with me. I just knew it did.

A few days later, I wandered into a secondhand bookshop, the kind that smelled like old paper and mildew, and a spine caught my eye.

The Collected Writings of the Marquis de Sade.

I opened it. Then slammed it shut. The pages were horrifying. Graphic. Depraved. Unhinged. How could someone write this filth, let alone publish it in the 18th century?

And yet...

The next night, I opened it again. This time, I read more slowly. Eyes wide. Heart pounding. Taking in every disturbing word, not as a victim, but as something else entirely, *"It is always by way of pain one arrives at pleasure,"* and *"In order to know virtue, we must first acquaint ourselves with vice."*

Then it came, that thought: What if that power wasn't used on me... but by me? Not because I agreed with the madness. Not because I found pleasure in the violence. But because for the first time, I imagined myself not crying on the floor... but standing above it. Not violated. In control.

I pictured the ones who had used me, shamed me, stolen from me. The ones who tried to erase me. And in my mind, I stood tall. Dignified. Composed. Holding the whip, not feeling it.

What began as a revenge fantasy became a doorway. Not a door into healing, into power. Into something that looked like control.

I began researching: BDSM. The Marquis. The underground world. What I found wasn't chaos, it was structure. Not brutality, but consent. Not healing, but ritualized power. There were rules. There was order. There was elegance.

This wasn't depravity, not in their eyes. It was art. Ceremony. Roleplay.

Online, I saw images of high-gloss latex, cages, surgical tables, crosses, floggers, and heels like weapons. But what captivated me wasn't the aesthetic... It was the code. The mutual understanding. The reverence for dominance. The sacredness of trust.

And something inside me whispered: You're not broken. You're becoming. I wasn't drawn to submission. Not even slightly. I didn't want to be tied down. I wanted to tie them. I didn't want to be told what to do. I wanted to dictate the rules with a cool glance and a gloved hand.

Contessa Doll wasn't a stage name. She was a summoning. Part vengeance. Part resurrection. She was everything that had been taken from me. Repackaged. Refined. Reclaimed.

She didn't cry over ruined childhoods or shattered dreams. She didn't flinch at cruelty. She became the thing that once terrified her.

"There is no God, nature suffices."

-De Sade

And if Nature made me a survivor, Contessa made me a sovereign. She wore pain like perfume. She didn't ask for respect; she commanded it. Because I was tired of being the one left on the floor, crying over motherhood lost. Over love betrayed. Over dreams crushed.

Contessa Doll rose. In heels. In leather. In command. And she was coming.

It didn't take long before I found myself at **The Hellfire Club**, Sydney's infamous underground BDSM party, held monthly beneath the glow of a full moon. Of course it was.

When the invitation came to perform a feature strip show, I said yes without hesitation.

I stepped onto the stage in a crisp, starch-white nurse's uniform, picture Nurse Ratched meets 80s slasher queen. Under the piercing lights, the crowd glowed: Dom's draped in latex and corsets, subs in collars and nothing else, towering men in leather harnesses, and the occasional business-suited voyeur, eyes wide, mouths agape.

Slowly, I drew a scalpel from my pocket and began slicing the uniform apart. Each cut was deliberate, as if I were cutting flesh instead of fabric. White lingerie peeked through, stained with crimson stage blood I smeared across my chest. The crowd howled.

Men gasped. Women purred. Doms gripped the leashes tighter. Subs strained forward to get a better look. I arched my back, dragged the blade down, and let my eyes blaze. That's when he approached.

Master Cage

Leather. Muscles. Hair bleached to defy nature and good taste. He looked like He-Man if He-Man had started a suburban dungeon and a tanning salon. *"I've never seen you here before,"* he smirked. *"That performance was... intense. Inspiration?"*

"80s slasher films," I shrugged. *"It's not that deep."*

He introduced himself, casually bragging about his home dungeon setup. And because I had zero self-preservation instincts, or maybe I just didn't care anymore, I accepted his invitation.

A week later, I was in his basement. It was cold. Clinical. Silent. No clutter. No chaos. Just stainless steel, symmetry, and order. I remember thinking, If I go missing, at least I wore something flattering. *"Take off your dress,"* he said gently. *"Nothing sexual. I want to show you the rack."*

The actual rack. He strapped me in slowly. Respectfully. His voice was calm, almost paternal. He explained every step, the mechanics, the sensations, the safe words. He was in control. But I felt... peaceful.

Then......crack.

The whip landed like lightning. My back lit up with pain. And for one sickening moment, I was ten again, beneath the Panopoulos boys' fists... Crack.

Back in the schoolyard. Surrounded by taunts. Being called things I didn't understand yet… Crack.

My sister lying. Anton sneering. Mikko laughing while shattering everything I'd hoped for. But I didn't run. I didn't beg. I whispered," *Keep going*".

Each strike tore open a buried memory. But this time, I was the one who chose it. I invited the pain. I allowed it. He paused. *"Are you okay?"*

I looked up, wet-eyed and grinning, *"What's wrong, Cage? Am I wearing you out?"*

His expression changed, admiration, maybe even fear, as he cracked harder until skin broke. Until I trembled, cried, and felt something leave my body that I didn't need anymore.

When it was over, I stood. Marked. Shaken. But unbroken. Empowered. This wasn't just roleplay. It wasn't just kink. It was a ritual.

Contessa Doll wasn't just a persona. She was a survivor. She didn't just wear pain. She wielded it.

That night, I rewarded myself with a Valium-Xanax cocktail and slept harder than I had in weeks. And somewhere in that deep, numb silence…

I believed I had finally found peace. But peace without Jesus is just a well-decorated prison. And I hadn't escaped yet.

Becoming Her

My meetings with Master Cage were like a weekly Pilates class, as if he were training me for something. And it was him who first suggested it: *"You ever thought about becoming a dominatrix?"*

I didn't hesitate. Didn't blink. Didn't even need to think. *"Yes. I'd love to."*

He didn't have to ask twice. It was like he'd read my soul before I even knew what was written on it. He told me he had friends, people who ran private dungeons and were looking for new girls. But not just any girl. A girl who **got it**. A girl who understood this wasn't about sex. It was about power and fantasy.

So, he trained me. This time, he was the one on the rack. And I was the one holding the whip. He taped an X on the wall and said, *"That's your target."* He gave me a whip to practice at home …then let me practice on him.

He taught me rhythm. Control. Precision. He showed me how to safely insert toys into his...let's just say, back door with the grace of a nurse and the confidence of a surgeon.

And all the while, he repeated his mantra: *"I never do anything to anyone I wouldn't let done to me."* And he meant it. He was one of the rare ones who walked the walk and got walked on, too.

When he thought I was ready, he took me to my first dungeon. He walked me in like a proud coach bringing in his undefeated champion.

The woman in charge, **The Dungeon Madame**, looked like a chain-smoking grandmother who'd dyed her hair black one too many times. She gave me a slow once-over, trying to hide the smirk crawling across her face. I must've looked like a brunette Barbie in a Halloween dominatrix costume, all stilettos and shiny black PVC, strutting in like I was about to conquer the world.

She didn't buy it. But she owed Cage a favour, so, reluctantly, she agreed to let me try. That was the last time I ever saw Master Cage.

Years later, I heard he'd died the way many in the lifestyle fear, Accidental asphyxiation during a solo session. Even seasoned professionals fall. And that was the first time BDSM reminded me: This was also a dangerous game. But I kept going because something had already been born inside me.

The **dungeon** wasn't like the strip clubs. In strip clubs, youth ruled. The newer, the thinner, the shinier the better. But in the dominatrix world? Age was power. Experience was currency. Wrinkles weren't flaws. They were battle medals. These women weren't playing princess. They were **Evil Queens**. Commanding. Unapologetically older. In their absolute prime. Some were in their 30s. Some in their 40s. Some in their 50s and 60s—walking tall in black lipstick and no fear.

And then there was **Mistress Steel.** A 50-year-old force of nature. Black fur coat. Long raven hair, sculpted into perfect 1950s vintage waves. Eyes that could freeze a man and make him apologize for being born.

One time, a man tripped, literally tripped through the dungeon entrance to get a glimpse of her.

Another time, I saw her step out of a luxury sports car, dropped off by the kind of silver-fox millionaire you'd expect to date Instagram models half his age. But he wasn't looking at them. He was looking at her. She stepped out, gave him a single nod, and walked away. He stayed. Just stood there. Watching her. Like a piece of his soul had detached and followed her in, I'll never forget it.

And I thought: That's the kind of power I want. That's the woman I want to become. Strong. Commanding.

Mysterious. Desired. Not despite her age, but because of it. And that was the moment she was truly born:

Mistress Contessa Doll. Not a broken girl. Not a model. Not a stripper. Not an escort. Not a porn star. But a woman with presence. A woman who didn't chase power - she embodied it. And soon, men would pay to kneel at her feet to taste a drop of what she'd survived.

Of course, I didn't get bookings at first. Few at all. I'd sit there in the dungeon's velvet waiting room, all black PVC and low lighting, while the seasoned Dom's sipped coffee brought to them by kneeling subs, smirking as they compared back-to-back sessions and bragged about which regulars were obsessed with them.

They laughed when I wasn't booked. Rolled their eyes like I was a charity case, just another ex-stripper playing pretend in patent leather. But I refused to give up. Not after everything I'd crawled through, not after what I'd survived. If I could endure all that, I could survive silence. I could outlast the smirks. I could sit through their shallow glances like a throne.

Then came the client no one wanted. A name that made even the toughest Dom's wince. An older man named **Mr Enzo.** With requests they called too vile, too extreme, too disgusting. Even the madame tried to steer him away. But I raised my hand. *"I'll take him,"* I said. *"If I must become the weirdo he's looking for, I will."*

He wasn't interested in touching me. Thank God. It was all about him. His fetishes. His fantasies. His filth. And they were revolting. But I leaned in. I locked eyes. And when he tried to shock me, I smiled and said: *"Delicious."*

He spewed depravity. I nodded like I was sipping tea. His fantasies sounded like something ripped from a banned VHS.

A box labelled: **Evidence Do Not Watch**. I didn't blink. I even recommended a few videos. *"Ever seen Live Leak? You'd love it."*

We watched them together. I feigned laughter. Spanked him. Fisted him. Smirked. Even purred: *"Oooh, that's hot."*

Just to watch his eyes light up. Like a Christmas tree in hell. And when Enzo left? He floated out of that dungeon like a man reborn. Five-star reviews followed. Not just to the madame, but to the other Dom's. To other clients. Word spread. *"She's a nice lady. She's a lot of fun."*

That was all it took. One glowing review from the client no one wanted, and suddenly, every head turned. Now the same women who once mocked me were asking: *"What did you do in there?"*

I just smiled. *"Whatever he needed. Nothing more. Nothing less."*

But I saw the shift. Felt it like heat on my skin. They were watching me rise. Because when every other Dom said no I stepped forward and said: *"I am danger."*

And they believed me. They had to. Because now, they saw me. Not the girl in heels playing pretend. But Mistress Contessa Doll. The woman who didn't blink. The woman who didn't break. The woman who said yes. When even the dungeon said no.

The Dungeon

Every dungeon follows the same blueprint: A cold, clean black room with toys hanging like steel jewellery on the walls: cuffs, chains, gags, harnesses, each one gleaming under dim, red-tinted lights. A mock medical clinic, fully stocked with sterile instruments that made clients squirm before we even touched them. A plush Victorian bedroom, for sessions that ended in more... intimate services. A classroom, sometimes converted into a chapel for roleplays with nuns, headmasters, and dirty little confessions.

There was the Pussy Parlour: a soft pink room full of satin and lace. It was the cross-dressing suite. A closet of wigs, makeup, corsets, pretty dresses, and heels, all man-sized, of course.

And then there was my favourite: The Red Room. The Red Room was sacred. A temple of fetish and fury. Bondage. Impact play. Sensory deprivation. A heavy wooden throne sat in the corner as if it ruled the room itself. Floggers, paddles, canes. Suspension hooks. CBT boards. Violet wands. Weapons of mass seduction and destruction. It was beautiful. It was terrifying. It was home.

And that's where I met the love of my life: Electroplay. The first time was with a client who wanted to be electrocuted. Another Dom was setting him up with pads, clips, and wires attached to places I won't list.

Then she turned to me, handed me the control unit, and said, *"Try it on yourself first. That's how you know it's set right."*

So, I did.

I pressed the button. What hit me wasn't a warm-up. No build. No tease. Just instant voltage cutting through skin, slicing past nerves, burrowing straight into bone. A delicious, agonising jolt. It was pure. No games. No mercy.

I gasped. And then I laughed. Because nothing had ever felt like that. Nothing had ever made me feel like that. From that moment on, the electrostim kit became my private ritual.

If I was sad, I'd hook myself up. If I was stressed, I'd turn it on. If I was happy, I'd reward myself with a session. It was my forbidden joy. Alone in the red glow, I'd cry and grin at the same time. Tears falling while my body danced beneath the current. The pain was like a drug.

And here's the part they never tell you about pain: Once you get past the agony... It becomes euphoria. It felt powerful. To take something that once destroyed me. And twist it into something pleasurable with my own hands. Not because someone told me to. Not to please. Not to earn. Not to survive. Because I chose it. Even in my most vulnerable state. I was still in control.

Strange thing about hurting men for money: I was starting to like them. I know how that sounds. But it's true. The dungeon stripped everything down.

Literally, yes. But also, emotionally. The mask slipped. The ego melted. And what was left underneath was... The real man.

That's when I realized: Men and women can heal each other. It makes sense, doesn't it? If we were created to fit together, to carry life, to continue the species... Then, of course, we were also designed to soothe each other's wounds. But ego gets in the way. On both sides. Stripping made me hate men. My past made me fear them. But BDSM... Made me love them again.

Because I finally saw them. Not the polished persona. Not the cocky voice or puffed-up pride. Just… them.

Women are lucky. We're allowed to cry together. To hold each other. Men? Men must pretend. To look invincible, even when they're falling apart. And then they came to the dungeon. Men who had been hurt. Violated. Desensitized. Angry. Silenced.

And because there was nowhere else for their pain to go. They coped however they could. Some became Dom's. Some became subs. Some just came to me and asked me to help them feel again.

That's when I stopped seeing them as clients and started seeing them as people. Hurting. Messy. People just like me.

Debbie's Warning

People don't realise how fast it goes. Not your relevance...your life. You think you've got time. Then you blink, and years have passed. One dungeon shifts after another. One month turning into the next. And just like that, another birthday.

But I wasn't slowing down. If anything, I was sharpening. My name was building. My presence in the room held weight. I wasn't fading, I was becoming. Still, one voice stayed with me.

Debbie

She was one of the old streetwalkers from Sydney's Kings Cross, the kind who wore the entire city on her face. Cigarettes, heartbreak, and eyeliner smudged by the years. Debbie had been in the game since she was a teenager. Ran from an abusive home, ended up in a girls' juvenile boarding house, and snuck out with a friend to chase something, anything that felt like freedom.

They found the Cross instead. It was the early 1980s. Neon signs. Strangers with promises. Danger wrapped in glamour. They were walking past a club when a bouncer called out, told them to come inside for an "**audition**." There was no audition. Just two young girls and a man who saw profit. They were given jobs and a room that night.

Debbie rose fast. Tall. Blonde. Radiant. Beautiful, she had that impossible combination, raw magnetism, and total vulnerability. Model features. A body made for the stage. A smile that made men forget themselves.

She became a feature dancer. A Penthouse Pet. She was flown to Japan, where they clapped when she stepped off the plane and threw parties in her honour. She was treated like royalty. They screamed her name when she danced.

But when she came home? They spat. No one wanted a girl from King Cross, let alone a stripper.

Fame doesn't follow you to the Cross. Only shame does, and that shame clung to her like mould. It seeped into her skin. She slipped into addiction, and it took her fast. The bookings dried up. Clubs started favouring newer, younger girls. She went from cover shoots to live sex shows, just to afford her next hit. Then it was the streets. Then it was survival.

She didn't just lose the work. She lost her glow. By the time I met Debbie, she was skeletal. Her legs were thin but still carried that echo of the dancer she once was. Her arms were wiry. Her skin hung loose across her stomach. Her teeth were mostly gone, but she still wore lipstick like she had somewhere important to be.

She dressed like she was still twenty, low-cut tops, short shorts, glitter belts, but her body told the truth. The drug use had carved it out. Made her hollow. Her cheeks were sunken. Her collarbones, sharp. She was mostly bones, nerves, and defiance.

And yet, she still had presence. She still had heart. She used to say that if she'd had a daughter, she would've left the life years ago. She would've tried. She would've fought.

Whenever I saw her working near my place, I'd stop and get her a coffee. Sit with her. Talk. She still looked out for the sex workers, no matter what industry we were in. According to Debbie, we were all in the same boat. And she was right.

She gave advice. Called everyone "**baby**" like she meant it. She'd seen the worst of the world, and she still tried to protect us from it. She'd lean in close and whisper: *"This industry will take your youth, your beauty, your fertility, your heart, and if you let it, your humanity."*

And then she'd say: *"Have an end goal, baby. Know when to get out."* I heard her. I did.

Her words branded me. But I couldn't take her advice. I had no ID. No way to study. No passport. No driver's licence. No access to anything beyond the world I was already in. I couldn't get out, not then. So, I stayed. And I started to wonder if I'd become her.

Then one day, I heard she'd passed. An overdose. Alone. Debbie, the girl they once celebrated. The woman who danced beneath lights and dreamed of protecting a daughter she never had. The one who looked after broken girls as if they were her own.

She died the way so many do in this world. Not with a bang. With a whisper. Forgotten by most. But not by me. I still hear her voice. *"Have an end goal, baby."* I just didn't know what mine was yet.

Trophy and Tired

It happened fast. Or maybe it just felt that way, like everything was moving in fast-forward and I'd only just caught up. I wasn't the best dominatrix in Australia, not by a long shot.

Maybe I was just different. Maybe it was the porn. Maybe the modelling history. Maybe it was the twisted, unfiltered things I said in session. Maybe it was the contrast of a beautiful face paired with a dark, sadistic soul. Whatever it was, it stuck.

My name started circulating. I was becoming more popular. I started winning awards. Sponsors wanted my name stamped on sex toys. Interviews started lining up. I took home another trophy at the Australian Adult Industry Awards **"Best Fetish Fantasy"**.

On the outside, I looked like I'd made it. On the inside, I was splitting at the seams. That same night, still high on adrenaline and cheap validation, I came home and checked my phone. Three missed calls. Two texts. I thought maybe someone was calling to congratulate me. Nope.

Contessa, where are you? We've got a client here asking for you. Four hours. He's been waiting all night.

Four hours. Four hours of whatever sick fantasy he'd paid for. I was supposed to be celebrating. Instead, I was throwing a Red Bull and my gear into a bag, squeezing into black PVC, and Ubering across the city to the bordello.

When the dungeon closed, a top-tier brothel picked me up straight away. They called it **"The Bordello"** like it was a brand. It looked like a five-star hotel and ran like one, too.

They had the best girls, the highest prices, and they didn't hire just anyone. These girls were next-level stunning, top models, centrefolds, globe-trotting goddesses. Insta baddies with millions of followers, who made it look like their lives were bankrolled by beauty brands and sponsors, not by what really happened behind the scenes... and most of them didn't want someone like me working alongside them.

But I got hired anyway. And before long, we were all friends... sort of.

I made good money at The Bordello. I brought in clients. Which meant I had more **"freedom"** than the others. But let's be real, freedom just meant I wasn't on the roster, but I was still on-call. Always! They didn't love me. They loved my profit margins.

After another long night, exhausted and twitchy, I got home and reached for my usual wind-down cocktail: Xanax and Valium. But nobody warns you what happens when the drugs stop working, when your body builds a tolerance to the only thing keeping you halfway human.

One Xanax. Nothing. Another Valium. Nothing. Another. Still wired. My cat wanted affection. I pushed her away, furious. I started pacing. Red-faced. Swearing at the walls. I didn't want to waste another pill, but I couldn't keep going like this. And when it finally hit, it hit too hard. I passed out. Woke up nearly a full day later, drenched in dread and regret, blinking at a screen full of missed calls.

Late again. *"Contessa, where are you???"* I popped a Duromine to get through it. I knew it would make my jaw clench and stomach cramp, but at least I'd be alert enough to swing a whip. I sat in the back of that Uber thinking, Is this it? Is this what I'm gonna be forever? Some hollowed-out woman fisting men for money?

The thought wasn't new. The anger was. It was the only emotion that could still break through the meds. Zoloft numbed everything else, grief, fear, guilt—but the rage, it burned. Hot. Sharp. Constant.

I'd look at the girls laughing in the break room, talking about uni, boyfriends, holidays, new cars, new houses, and moving on. And today... I hated them for it. They had exit plans. I had chains and a room full of toys with my name engraved on them.

One night on break, one of the new girls, young, nervous, fresh-faced, too innocent to be here, tiptoed over. She needed to borrow my room for a quick session. Everything else was booked. She needed the money for uni. She reminded me of me. The me that had dreams. The me that still thought she'd be out in six months.

"Fine," I snapped. *"But make it quick. And don't you dare touch my equipment."* I meant it.

After my break ended, I checked the room. It was clean. Bed made. Everything where it should be, except for one of my whips, laid across the table like a threat. Not where I'd left it. It had been touched. I took a breath. And saw red. Stormed into the change room. Found her. Grabbed her by the arm and shoved the whip in her face. *"I told you not to touch my shit!"* I screamed.

Her eyes widened, terrified. She tried to explain. I didn't want to hear it. I was past reason. Past grace. *"Are you an idiot? Don't fucking listen? I said Don't touch my stuff!"*

She stammered something about the client wanting to look at it. Said she never used it. Didn't matter. It wasn't about the whip. It was about everything. Every missed night of sleep. Every fake orgasm. Every man who called me

Mistress while secretly wishing I was dead. Every award and envelope full of money that didn't fix a thing.

I kept screaming. My grip on her arm tightened. Her lip trembled. She started crying. The other girls gathered. Some looked shocked. Some smirked. Entertained. I didn't care.

Dior (my brothel bestie) saw the commotion and rushed over. Pulled me away. The girl went home in tears. Too shaken to finish her shift. She needed the money. But I'd broken her. And I didn't feel bad. Because she had a future, she had a way out. I didn't. So I screamed. I punished her. I let the rage take over. Because if I was going to rot here forever, someone else was going to pay for it too.

"*Calm down,*" Dior said, thick American accent slicing through the tension. "*We've got a party booking together. My regular. I told him all about you—we're gonna have so much fun.*" She pointed to her nose, grinning.

Dior was one of my closest friends at The Bordello, on and off the clock. But it hadn't always been that way. We'd known each other for years and hated each other. Petty online drama, full-blown arguments, name-calling, threats. When she found out I was coming to The Bordello, she protested. Said I'd cheapen the place. Bring in the wrong crowd.

When I heard that, I vowed I'd make her life a living hell. And I was going to, until we met face to face. We got booked together. One shared session. That was all it took. They talk about love at first sight. Or enemies to lovers. For me and Dior, it was enemies to soul sisters in under an hour. The banter. The way we both held firm with clients. The unspoken understanding that we were the same kind of broken.

After our first session together, she asked why I called myself **Contessa Doll**. *"Well, my name's Tessa, and these are my dolls,"* I said, tossing a bag of pills onto the bed.

Dior laughed. *"Girl, if those are your dolls, then we should play Barbies,"* she said, tossing hers down too.

We both cracked up. That was it. Bond sealed. Same dependency. Different prescriptions. Same demons. Sometimes we traded. She told me which doctors to go to. Reminded me to get blood tests so I wouldn't accidentally overdose. Dior had a heart. She could find humour in anything—even this.

She also had a thing for plastic surgery. I never understood it. She was stunning. A living Jessica Rabbit, bright red hair, big green eyes, full lips, a body that stopped traffic. She made her own dresses, too. Always the best outfits in the whole Bordello, and she looked incredible outside of work too. People stared wherever she went.

But it was her beauty, it was her energy that lit the room. Still, she never thought she was enough. After her regular passed out during a three-hour session, coke and painkillers hitting harder than expected, Dior and I lay on the bed in white bathrobes, staring up at the mirrored ceiling. High as satellites. Just floating. She turned her head and said, *"That's not like you, Tess. What was that outburst about? You're not that petty. Over a whip? You're gonna get fired."*

I laughed. *"Good,"* I said. *"I don't care."* But I did. Because without ID, I couldn't get a license. Couldn't check into hotels. Couldn't work independently. And I sure as hell didn't want to work from home or downgrade to a cheaper brothel.

"Why are you so angry?" Dior asked, lighting a cigarette.

I sat up and told her everything. How I felt trapped. How I saw myself as an elderly dominatrix, still fisting clients for money. How my family didn't help me get my ID back. How this felt like the end of the road. She squeezed my hand and said, *"You don't know what tomorrow will bring. Don't worry, honey. The universe will find a way."*

I hoped she was right. But I wasn't sure I believed it.

Numb

Dragging myself to the bordello for a pre-booked shift, I already knew this client had paid in advance, so I knew the pervert was eager. No specific requests. He just said he was a first-timer.

That usually meant one thing: some older guy who's had it all, done it all, burned through every **normal** kink and now needed things to go a bit harder. I dealt with those all the time.

But when I opened the door, I froze. He wasn't some jaded old man. He was a boy—barely eighteen. In fact, he'd turned eighteen just a couple weeks prior. Shy. Awkward. Standing there like he was lost, maybe on his way to one of the other girls for a soft service, and knocked on my door by mistake.

No. This was no mistake. This was his birthday present to himself.

He told me he'd never tried BDSM before, but he knew it was **for him**. I asked if he was sure. If he really understood what he was getting into. I even tried to intimidate him, pulled out one of the more invasive, scary, painful-looking toys I owned.

He didn't flinch. He told me he'd had a **softer** service with one of the other girls a week prior, and he was bored. His first time? *"Dull"*

He said he'd been watching porn since he was a kid. Normal stuff didn't do it for him anymore. He needed harder. More extreme. He told me normal sex just didn't feel right, exciting. Then he said something that turned my blood cold.

He said I could do whatever I wanted to him, anything at all, just don't kiss him on the lips. He was saving that for his first girlfriend. He was willing to be humiliated, dominated, and tortured, but he hadn't had his first kiss yet. Not even a chance to fall in love.

I looked him in the eye and said, *"If this is what you're into now… what are you going to do to a girlfriend later?"*

And I thought about Anton, my first boyfriend in high school, how he'd treated me, how I was just a toy to him. Nothing real. Nothing sacred. Just flesh. Just porn come to life. And suddenly, I saw it. I wasn't part of the solution. I was part of the problem. I took a breath because that kid wasn't the only one.

More of my clients were getting younger and asking for things they'd seen online. Extreme things. Torture. The most perverse requests you could imagine. Stuff that shouldn't even be legal, let alone considered sexy. And I realized I wasn't helping anyone. I was making it worse. Worse for some girl out there who'd be just like me at seventeen. Who'd have to deal with boys already broken by porn? A girl who'd never get to be loved before being used. And I was the person making sure that happened.

Something shifted. I didn't have the language for it yet, but I felt it, low and sharp, like dread curling in the pit of my stomach. Not guilt. Not grief. Just a quiet, creeping truth I couldn't outrun anymore. No one saw it coming. One day, the world was normal.

Shift

The 2020 lockdown hit like a thief in the night. One minute, I was booked solid back-to-back, weeks ahead. The next, the whole world stopped. Cold.

Brothels were shut down. Private work became impossible. We couldn't see clients without risking fines or arrest. Even if a client was willing to book, it was never worth the risk. During an international, deadly pandemic, sex workers weren't allowed to work, not legally, not without risk. And I had nothing to fall back on, no ID, no government assistance, no family support, no safety net. I started draining my savings, hoping each week would be the last.

It wasn't. It dragged on. And on. And on. I started hurting myself more, just to feel something other than dread. Even pain felt better than that. But that didn't work either. The dread was so thick it became its own sound, like white noise in my brain. No clarity. No light. Just fog and static and the sinking feeling that I was disappearing inside myself.

I shut down. Stopped replying. Ignored messages. Switched off the world. I didn't even have the energy to pretend I was okay. By the time lockdown finally lifted, there was barely anything left of me, money, motivation, or mind. I dragged myself back to work. Hollow. Kind of dead inside. I walked into the brothel and barely looked at the receptionist. *"I'm so sorry,"* she said.

I paused, confused. *"For what?"*

"I heard… Dior passed away."

No. No fucking way. Not Dior. My Dior. My brothel bestie. My spark. My sister in sin. Gone. Overdose during lockdown. She'd messaged me. I didn't reply. I saw the messages, but I was too deep in it. Too numb. Too ghost-like. I told myself I'd write back when I felt better. But I never did.

There was no funeral. No public post. No tribute. Just a whisper through the grapevine. When I finally found out where she was buried, I went. It was a flat grave marker—just her name, birth, and death. No headstone. No sequins. No sparkle. No sign she ever lit up a room. Just dirt. Like she'd never existed. The only colour was the flowers I laid down myself. I stood there shaking my head. *"It's not her,"* I whispered. But it was.

That was her body, once magnetic, beautiful, the body she'd poured so much money into trying to perfect, now buried in silence. Decaying in dirt that didn't deserve her.

I was already spiraling, running on fumes, when the next Australian lockdown hit. If 2020 was the earthquake, 2021 was the tsunami. It didn't just destroy; it wiped everything away. I had no money. No plan. The walls started closing in. I felt trapped. Dread. That kind of dread where your skin feels too tight for your bones. It was like living inside a nightmare with no off switch. Just dread. Just survival. Just white knuckling it through every hour.

And then one night, I heard it. A sound from downstairs. A howl. At first, I thought I was imagining it. Then I heard it again. And my stomach dropped. I knew that sound. I ran. There she was, Mama. My sweet, loving, snuggly little cat. Collapsed on her side. Tongue out. Legs twitching. Barely breathing. I screamed. I panicked. I called 000, choking on my own voice.

The woman on the line sounded annoyed. *"We don't handle animals,"* she snapped. *"Only humans."* I dropped.

Posted on Facebook, begging for help. Shaking so hard I could barely type. My hands were trembling so badly I could barely hold the phone. A friend messaged and told me there was a 24-hour vet nearby.

I wrapped Mama in a towel, whispering, *"Don't die, don't die, don't die,"* repeatedly in the Uber. The vet told me she was brain-dead. They had to put her to sleep. There was no other option. They asked if I wanted to leave the room. No. She would see me when she went. Not a stranger. Not a vet in a mask. Me. I held her face against mine and watched the heart monitor fade to black.

In the waiting room, I cradled her little body in a towel like a newborn. Her fur still smelled like home. Her warmth fading by the second.

I had so much medication in my system, antidepressants, sleeping pills, benzos, diet meds, but I couldn't cry. I couldn't feel anything. And I couldn't help but wonder, was I so out of it that I didn't notice my cat was sick? Or was she hiding it? Still trying to comfort me, even as she was dying?

The grief slammed into something inside me, but it couldn't break through. It was stuck. Muffled. Like screaming underwater. Something cracked. I started hyperventilating. My chest seized. My throat closed. I wanted to cry, but it was like the part of me that knew how had been shut off. The sadness just hit the wall and bounced back. Repeatedly. Trapped.

I picked up the phone and called my sister, not because I trusted her, not because I thought she'd care, but because I was falling apart, and maybe, just maybe, someone in the family would finally find it in their heart to show up. She didn't. She told me to calm down. *"It's just a cat."*

Then my dad called. She'd clearly rung him, played the concerned sibling role. He didn't ask if I was okay. He never did. He told me I sounded crazy. Said I could buy another cat tomorrow. Told me to pull myself together. Then he hung up.

Just a cat? Mama wasn't just a cat. She was my constant. My comfort. My witness. She curled up next to me after I'd been torn apart in my toxic marriage. She purred on my belly when I knew motherhood was gone for me. She waited at the door after brutal sessions. She was there when Dior died. She was there when lockdown hit. She was there when no one else was. And now she was gone.

My chest clamped down. My breathing got faster. I couldn't stop it. Couldn't slow it. Then... flashing lights. Voices. A stretcher. The paramedics were there.

Next thing I know, I'm waking up in a hospital bed. A doctor with kind eyes leaned over me. *"I lost my cat,"* I whispered. *"She died."*

She nodded. *"I cried more when my dog died than when my father passed,"* she said. *"That kind of love... It's different. It's real. It's unconditional."* She was right.

Mama was love. Pure. Loyal. Simple. Steady.

The doctor said the vet called an ambulance because they were worried about me. My breathing. The way I was processing grief, or how I wasn't. She told me what I already knew but hadn't said out loud. I was on a dangerous mix of meds: antidepressants, benzos, sleeping pills, and diet pills. And sometimes I mixed them with party drugs just to get through a shift. It was only a matter of time.

She said gently but firmly: Go to your GP. Start weaning off. If you keep going like this, you won't last much longer before I end up just like Dior. A flat marker. A name and a date.

That was the moment I knew: I had to get off the meds. All of them. The antidepressants. The benzos. The diet pills. The cocktail that kept me going but never healing. Because I wasn't grieving like a person anymore. I wasn't feeling. And it wasn't pain I was trying to avoid. I'd lived with pain. Worked in pain. That was never the problem. What I was avoiding was emotion. I was skipping them like they were optional. Like I could medicate my way around them. But grief is meant to be felt. And I didn't want to choke on it anymore.

I wanted to weep. I wanted to scream. I wanted to let the sadness out instead of swallowing it whole, so I started the slow, terrifying detox. After years of drugging myself into numbness, I wanted to feel again. Not just sadness. Not just heartbreak. Everything. Even if it broke me. Even if it scared the hell out of me. I didn't know who I'd be when the fog lifted. But whoever she was… She'd be real.

Pain and Other Forms of Cruelty

Nobody tells you what it's going to feel like when you come off a cocktail of tranquilizers and antidepressants. Nobody warns you that it won't just feel like the floor's been ripped out, it'll feel like your entire brain is being electrocuted, rewired, rewound.

It wasn't just the physical withdrawal. It was a collapse from the inside out. When you've shoved emotions behind walls for years, shoved them down, numbed them, medicated them into silence, they don't crawl back quietly. They erupt. Explode. They don't ask permission. They don't knock. They kick the door in and flood the place like a riot. There's no order. No sequence. Just pure, violent emotional carnage.

I wasn't remembering things; I was being ambushed by them. Memories didn't drift in gently; they came with fists. Screaming. Clawing. Flashbacks. Guilt. Hurt. Betrayal. Regret. Sadness. Shame. All of it detonated at once.

And my body? My body betrayed me in every possible way. The brain zaps felt like lightning bolts behind my eyes, like someone was hitting me with a cattle prod inside my skull. My muscles ached so deeply that it felt like they were splitting open from the bone. My jaw locked up. My limbs twitched. My heart would race like I was running from something, then crash like I was dying. I couldn't sleep. When I did doze off, I'd wake up drenched in sweat, gasping, shaking, or sobbing for reasons I couldn't name. My skin felt like it was crawling. My chest would tighten so hard I thought I was having a heart attack. Then nothing. Then terror. Then nothing again.

I'd wake up stiff as a corpse, body aching like I'd been hit by a truck in my sleep.

If it weren't for Uber Eats, I wouldn't have eaten. I couldn't move. Couldn't think. Couldn't even speak properly. I probably would've died in that apartment, and nobody would've noticed, not until the landlord came banging on the door asking for his rent.

Some girl online said cannabis helped her through withdrawals. She gave me a number for a doctor. I didn't hesitate. I was too desperate to care. I got it. Used it. And yeah, it helped. Not a cure. Not clarity. But enough to slow down the madness so I could breathe.

But from the outside? I must've looked insane. Eyes darting, years of tears bursting out mid-sentence. Maybe I was unhinged. Maybe the drugs had been the only thing keeping the dam from bursting. But I didn't care. I just needed the grief, the panic, the spiraling memories to slow the hell down.

I stopped eating. My ribs stuck out. My clothes hung off me like wet rags on a scarecrow, eating became physically impossible.

Friends in the industry, if you could even call people that at that point, came circling like vultures. *"Wanna shoot for our OnlyFans?"* *"We'll pay you."* Not much. Just enough to pay a bill or buy groceries.

That's when it hit me: they didn't give a single f*** about me. Just what I could still do for them. As long as I was usable, I was valuable. The moment I wasn't? I didn't exist.

And somewhere in all of that madness, I noticed the silence. Mama cat was gone.

I wasn't healed. I wasn't even functional. But the quiet wrapped around me. So, I went to the shelter and adopted another shattered little soul. **Button**. A former feral. Her first litter had been stomped to death by neighbourhood children. When the shelter found her, she was pregnant again. After her kittens had all been adopted out, they told me she just needed love.

So, did I. Two broken hearts, barely beating. That's what we were. But she didn't trust me. She wouldn't come near me. Wouldn't purr. Wouldn't cuddle. She shook in the corner, watching me like I might turn on her. Like I was just another monster. Another human she had to outlast.

I didn't blame her. I didn't try to force it. I just gave her food. Space. Soft places to land. I didn't want to pressure her. I just wanted her to be less afraid. Then, out of nowhere.....The landlord sold the building.

I had thirty days. No savings. No ID. Not even a car to sleep in. Where was I supposed to go? What was I going to do with Button after dragging her off the streets? Was I about to throw her back onto them? I spiraled. I was about to be homeless.

I started packing in a rage, flinging things into boxes as if by smashing enough of the past, it would finally shut up. But it didn't. Old photos surfaced. Old wounds reopened. My sister. My family. The cruelty. The betrayal. The years of pretending I was fine.

I messaged her. Unleashed everything. Years of repressed pain. The abuse. The silence. The guilt she never owned. The damage she denied. She left me on read.

So, I sent another. And another. Then my father called. Yelling. Accusing. *"Why are you raving like a lunatic?"* he said. And I told him. Everything. What I'd been through. What I'd done to survive. That all I ever needed, ever, was a single piece of paper. An ID. Proof I existed. Something that could've spared me years of selling my body to survive. I thought maybe, just maybe, he'd understand. Instead, he sent me a thousand dollars. Like that was going to fix it. Like my life was an invoice he could pay off and forget.

Then I found out from one of my sister's baby daddies, of all people, that she'd been spinning this story for years. Telling everyone I was a drugged-out prostitute. That I blew every dollar on narcotics. That I was better off out of their lives. Safer far from her children. Unworthy. Unfixable.

And for years, years, my sister had been poisoning my dad's mind and anyone who'd listen. Whispering lies. That I was unstable. Dangerous. A burden. And they believed her without asking my version. She told everyone not to help me. Said I needed to suffer to learn. That giving me help would only feed my destructive behaviour. And they believed her. Nodded along. Smiled their fake sympathy smiles while stepping over my suffering.

I called my dad again. Hoping there was still some version of him left—some sliver of the man I used to love. I told him the truth that I wasn't high. That I was surviving. That I was doing my best in the middle of a global f***ing pandemic. And then he said it. *"Listen, I'm not one of those men who stick their c*** in your mouth for money. Tell me the truth. What are you doing with the money?"* I froze.

That sentence shattered something in me that will never fully grow back. I told him he was no better than the clients who paid to hurt me. I reminded him he faked a suicide note just to run off with some young South African tart that he abandoned us. Lied. Blamed his own children.

And then I told him this... *"At least the men who paid me never pretended to love me"*

That was the last time I ever spoke to him. I slammed my front door. My skin was burning. My face was hot with rage and humiliation. I stormed through the city like a bomb that didn't go off. The place that once felt like a sanctuary now looked grey. Flat. Cold. Dead.

I walked past masked families on picnic blankets, laughing like the world wasn't crumbling. Pretending this was still life. Why didn't I have that? I didn't want riches. I didn't want fame. I just wanted a family. A child. Someone to call me Mum. Someone to raise and nurture. Someone to hold. Was that too much to ask? Was I cursed just for dreaming it?

Later that night came the knock. Police. My sister had called them. Said I was unwell. Said no one had heard from me in days, that I was spiraling. That I was a threat. I explained it was a family dispute. Showed them the call logs. One of the officers even suggested I get a restraining order. Said she'd been harassing the station for days.

I called a mutual friend. Asked if he had a room at his boarding house. He said yes. Relieved, I thought maybe, maybe I'd caught a break. Then he called back.

End of My Rope

I've had a few suicide attempts in my past, none of them worked. I always woke up in a hospital bed, confused and angry to still be breathing. But this time was different. This time, I knew I had to succeed.

Because if I woke up again, I wouldn't have a home to go back to. I had no money, no ID, no job, no family. I was going to be homeless. And that wasn't a hypothetical; it was coming fast. There was no safety net. No one coming to save me.

I sat on the stairs, lights off. My insides matched the room: cold, black, empty. I wasn't crying anymore, not really. My eyes were raw, but the tears weren't sadness. They were the body's last flicker. I remember thinking, *"I get it now. I'm not meant to survive this. That's why everything's been so hard. That's why every door slammed shut. Every wall I hit. Every prayer to the universe that fell flat. It was all leading here"*.

This was the end. And it made sense. It almost felt peaceful. I went to my BDSM toolkit and pulled out the black rope. The one I'd used for years, wrapping it around the bodies of clients, tying it into beautiful, cruel shapes. Tonight, it was just one shape—a noose.

I tied it to the banister at the top of the stairs. When I jumped, it would be enough. Enough to make sure I didn't wake up this time.

I held the noose up and looked through it like a window. On the other side, I imagined freedom. I saw Dior. I saw Mama Cat. I saw all the people I'd lost, waiting. And I felt... relief like I was finally about to clock out of a job I never wanted in the first place.

I slipped the noose over my neck. I stood on the edge of the banister barefoot. Took a deep breath. And then, just as I started to lean forward, I heard something. Not out loud. Not in the room. It was a voice buried in the back of my mind. Like a sermon I didn't know I still remembered. *"If you repent on the last, you won't go to hell."*

Some old pastor from the Christian Brethren days. I used to roll my eyes in those services. But right then, dangling at the edge, I remembered it... Hell. That's probably why my other attempts never worked. Deep down, I still believed in hell. And as bad as this life was, what if that place was worse? I froze.

Then I climbed back down. I collapsed on the stairs, crying, sobbing. Not the kind of tears that beg for help, but the kind that come when you've already given up. I prayed, if you could even call it that. *"God... I get it. I know I deserve this. I know why I'm here. I know what I've done. But if there's anything left in You, any tiny scrap of mercy, please forgive me for what I'm about to do. I can't stay here. I can't survive this. So, when I go, please let me be with them, with my loved ones on the other side. Please don't send me to hell. I've suffered enough."*

I stood up again. Climbed back over the banister. My fingers curled around the edge. I was ready this time. I took a deep breath. Just as I started to let go, I felt something. Not imagined. It felt real. It wrapped firmly around my waist like arms of warmth. I didn't see it. I didn't need to. I felt it. Like a hug. Like someone who had been waiting for me this whole time. Watching me self-destruct. Missing me. And now, finally, I'd called out. I heard it, clear as day, not in my ears, but in my spirit. *"You're going to be okay. I'm here. I've got you."*

I broke. *"I've made a mess,"* I whispered. *"There's no way out of this."*

But the voice came again, steady. *"You're going to be okay. I never left you."*

"What do I do?" I asked.

"Open the Bible."

I almost laughed. The Bible? The one I used as a prop in nun role-playing sessions? The one used to hit clients during humiliation sessions? That Bible? But I did it anyway. I opened it. And the first word I saw? Mark. And I knew.

My friend Mark. I hadn't spoken to him in a while. The one who always posted roommate ads. The one who didn't know my sister didn't buy into rumors—the one who might, just maybe help.

I grabbed my phone and called him, still tangled in sobs and snot and shaking fingers. I told him everything. The rope. The stairs. The eviction. The end. He listened. Then he said, *"Pack your stuff. You're coming here. You're going to be ok."*

I could barely breathe. Could barely stand. After we hung up, I flipped through the Bible again. Not searching, just turning pages. And then I saw it.

Prostitute

I froze. Wait...what? There's a prostitute in the Bible? I thought it was just pure virgins and perfect saints. But no. Her name was Rahab. She was a sex worker. And she wasn't just some side character. She was in the lineage of Jesus.

I sat with that. God didn't make a mistake when He made me. He saw me. All these years. Through every mask, every whip, every overdose, every client. Through the scenes and the screaming and the silence. He saw me. And He waited. He waited for me to stop running.

He waited like the father in that story, the prodigal son, standing at the edge of the road, scanning the horizon for the first sign of His lost child coming home. And....He ran to me. No lecture. No list of all the ways I'd failed. Just open arms. Ready to catch me.

Resurrected

The rebuild was slow. Painfully slow. Like trying to glue together a mirror that had been smashed, stepped on, and buried. But it was still a rebuild. And that was the miracle. Then out of nowhere: a phone call. The number was unfamiliar, but the voice on the other end stopped my heart. A voice I hadn't heard in years.

It was Mum. She didn't waste time. *"What's this I hear about you being in trouble?"* Her voice was tight, half-worried, half-judging. *"Your sister's been calling everyone, saying you're a porn star. A streetwalker. A heroin addict. That you've been in prison. That you're living in a homeless shelter, she told people not to send you money because you'd spend it on drugs. What's going on? Tell me yourself."*

So, I did. I told her everything. I didn't sugarcoat it. I didn't soften it to protect her. I told her about the porn, the prostitution, the BDSM, the drugs, the clients, and the years I spent pretending I was in control while I was silently breaking. I poured it out like a confession I didn't even know I'd been holding. She didn't interrupt. She didn't gasp or hang up. She just listened.

Then she exhaled, deep and slow, and said the one thing I'd waited my whole life to hear: *"How do I get you out?"*

Not Why did you do it? Not what were you thinking? Just: How do I help you leave? I said, *"Mum, I need my ID. That's all. I can't do anything without it."*

Mum didn't know where to start, but she started anyway. She walked into a Perth library, found a staff member behind a computer, and said, *"My daughter in Sydney needs help getting her identification."*

They helped her fill out forms, upload documents, and even wrote an email to the Department of Home Affairs on our behalf. We got the paperwork together. Legal Aid gave us a lawyer. And then it happened. I had ID.

Just a plastic card, but in Australia, without it, you're legally invisible. You can't study. You can't rent a home. You can't access government assistance. You can't apply for most jobs. You can't open anything official. You're trapped.

I lay on my bed and sobbed. Not just from relief, but from grief. Grief for all the things I'd lost. For all the years I'd lived in limbo. For the girl who needed help ten years earlier but had no one. For every opportunity I'd missed. Every door that wouldn't open. Every time I was told, Sorry, you need an ID for that.

I cried for the life I could've had. For the me that might've existed if someone had just stepped in sooner. And then, through the tears, I felt something warm curl up on my stomach. It was Button. My little trauma survivor. Once a feral cat who'd flinched at everything, now crawling onto me like a warm, soft teddy bear. She purred and pressed into me like it was her mission. I like to think God whispered to her, *"Go comfort her. Let her know I see her."*

I was renting a small room at Mark's place in an unfamiliar town, far from everything I'd ever known. No job. No savings. On government benefits. Detoxing from prescription meds. No idea who I was outside the sex industry. Just a shattered nervous system and a Bible, I barely knew where to start.

I started going to Hillsong. It was clean. Polished. The music felt like something from a stadium tour. The messages were nice, but it felt more like a show than a sanctuary. Still, I went. I needed routine. I needed structure. I needed to look forward to something every week. I needed to do something other than sit around the house doing nothing.

Then a COVID outbreak hit the church, and it temporarily shut down again. Doors closed. Livestreams started. Community disappeared. And the loneliness came back.

So, I went walking to clear my mind. That's when I heard it, a voice echoing through outdoor speakers in a local neighbourhood, *"YOU BELONG HERE."*

I turned toward the sound. It was a church, but not the kind I'd grown up in. There were colourful signs, fairy lights, and a kids' play area with a bouncy castle. It didn't look religious. It looked alive.

I lingered by the gate. I heard the pastor say something about worshipping together. That was all I needed. I told myself, Next week, I'll go in. No talking. No eye contact. Just sit in the back. Hear the sermon. Leave.

The next Sunday, I walked through the gates. A group of people turned, smiled, and waved. My stomach flipped. I panicked, pulled out my phone, pretended to be on a call, and started to walk away. Then a man gently tapped my arm. *"Is this your first time at Echo Church?"*

I nodded. *"Welcome,"* he said, smiling like it was no big deal. And that was it. No fake cheer. No pressure. Just kindness.

The sermon hit different. No fluff. No sugar. Just truth. Honest, raw, punch-in-the-gut kind of truth. The kind I never got in the Brethren church I grew up in, where sermons felt more like silent judgments than invitations to grace.

After the service, the lead pastor's wife came up and introduced herself. She asked, *"What brought you here? What's your testimony?"* I froze.

Later that day, I told Mum. I told her I liked the church, but I wasn't ready to tell them everything. I didn't want to become **that girl.** The former sex worker with the past no one knows how to handle. I didn't want polite pity or people looking with disdain.

Mum didn't miss a beat. *"Tell them the truth. And if they judge you, leave. But stop hiding."*

So, I went back. After the sermon, the lead pastor's wife, who is a pastor herself, found me again. Same question. This time, I answered. The porn. The brothels. The pills. The BDSM. The suicide rope. The shame. I didn't hold back. I laid it all out, raw and trembling. And when I finished, bracing for the shift in her eyes. She didn't flinch.

She said, *"You are none of those things now. You are a child of God."* Then she hugged me. A real hug. Not the one-armed, awkward kind. A full, tight, I-see-you kind of hug.

That was the moment I knew I'd found home. I started going to Wednesday night Bible study. Got to know the families. Their kids. Their stories. Their testimonies. Not everyone was born into the church. We all had different paths that led us to Jesus.

One Sunday morning, a little girl passed me on her way to the kids' ministry and said sweetly, *"Hello, Tessa."* It hit me like a sweet punch to the chest.

Tessa.

Not Contessa. Not Doll. Not Mistress. Just… me. I barely held it together. A woman in my row handed me tissues. She probably thought the sermon got to me.

After the service, I told one of the mothers that I used to work in childcare back in my teens. She said, *"You'd be amazing on the kids' ministry team."*

No judgment. No hesitation. Just trust. So, I said yes. I applied for a Working With Children Check, which in Australia is a legal background clearance everyone needs before working or volunteering with minors. It checks for criminal history, charges, and anything that might pose a risk to children. I passed easily. I had no convictions. No jail time. No record. Clean.

Life finally became peaceful. Not boring. Just peaceful and healing. I went back to study and finished my Certificate III, Australia's equivalent of a high school diploma or GED. It's the qualification you need to access most vocational training, apprenticeships, and entry-level jobs. For someone like me, who'd spent years without ID or stability, that certificate meant everything.

I worked part-time in hospitality. Took solo Bible study trips to small towns. Journaled by the lake. Walked around a nearby national park, took in the amazing views, and

Prayed. Sat with God. And loved those Sunday school kids like they were my own. Any old client who messaged me? I told them straight: *"I'm not in the business anymore."*

That one sentence had more power than any whip I ever held. The bordello called a few times, too. People were still asking for me. I told them to delete my number. And aside from Mum, I cut off the rest of my family, not out of hatred, out of peace. I forgave. But I didn't forget. I gave the rest to God.

Then one Sunday, I posted a photo on Instagram. Just one. It was a group shot, my Sunday school class and I. Bright sun. Big smiles. Wholesome. Normal. I didn't think much of it. People post life updates all the time when they leave the sex industry, new jobs, new partners, new babies. I was no different, right?

Two days later, the phone rang. It was a journalist. She asked if I was a Sunday school teacher now. I said yes. Then came the questions: *"Does your church know your past?"* *"Are you celibate?"* *"Are you seeing anyone?"*

She sounded casual. Friendly. I didn't think much of it. That Sunday morning, serving in the kids ministry, my phone wouldn't stop buzzing. At first, I thought it was Mum. Then I saw the texts. *"I'm so sorry. Are you okay?"* *"Have you seen this?"* *"Is this true?"*

I clicked the link. There it was. Photos of me in black lingerie, holding a whip, side-by-side with a photo of me in my Sunday school uniform.

Headlines read:

FROM DOMINATRIX TO SUNDAY SCHOOL TEACHER.

It was everywhere: the Daily Mail, the New York Times, and the front page of the Midweek Sport UK. Blogs. Forums. Social media. One article even said I'd become a nun. Others completely twisted my story. Some people were outraged. Others made jokes. A few asked why I was allowed near children and questioned the church's integrity. Like my testimony was some punchline or worse, a threat.

I went cold. I excused myself and locked myself in the church bathroom. This is it, I thought. This is the end of me in kids' ministry. Not only are they judging me, they're judging the church for trusting me. A mother walked out of the stall and saw my face. I showed her the article. She didn't even blink. *"You've been honest with us from day one,"* she said. *"It's going to be okay."*

After class, I went straight to the pastor's wife. Showed her everything. She read it, looked me in the eye, and said, *"We've got your back. Echo gets media attacks all the time. We're used to it. You'll get through this. Jesus is walking it with you, and so are we."*

And they did. The church didn't flinch. They backed me publicly. They stood up for me behind closed doors. Anyone who questioned my role in kids' ministry was reminded that this is what grace looks like.

But that night? I broke. I sobbed. Hard. God, why would You let this happen? This is every ex–sex worker's nightmare. My story is viral. My testimony is clickbait. My life is a joke.

And in the stillness, I heard it in my spirit: You've survived worse. You're still living. Your church still loves you. I didn't bring you this far to abandon you. Everything will turn around for God's glory.

That changed everything. I wasn't going to run. I wasn't going to be ashamed. Yes, that was me. But I don't live there anymore. And if they were going to make me a headline? Then they were going to get the whole story!!!

Soon after, something incredible happened. Sex workers, past and present, started messaging me. Some said they'd started praying. Some said they felt hope for the first time. Others said they were afraid to leave the industry, but my story gave them courage.

That's when I realised. This wasn't a punishment. It was a platform. And I was going to use it.

I started speaking out. Podcasts. Interviews. Panels. Eventually, I started co-hosting a show. I told the truth about the industry. The part nobody glamorises. The reality of men who get so desensitized by porn that nothing soft or intimate turns them on anymore, only degradation. Only violence. I'd seen it. I'd profited from it. I knew what it did to them, and to me.

Now, once a month, I go back into brothels. Not to work, but to do outreach. With a team of women who give up their time to help sex workers. We talk. We listen. We pray. We connect them with services. We remind them: They are loved and valued. There is a way out. Because God can redeem anything.

It felt slow when I was crawling through it. But now, looking back, I see how fast He moved, and I barely recognise that woman in those provocative photos holding a whip. But I don't reject her.

Contessa Doll is part of my testimony. And I'm not ashamed of her. Jesus didn't save the perfect version of me.

Tessa Williams

For years, Tessa was known as Contessa Doll, a leading name in the Australian adult industry. She won awards, gained national recognition, and achieved the kind of status many in that world chased. Yet behind the glamour, she battled depression, self-harm, and the crushing reality of feeling trapped in a life she no longer wanted.

When the isolation of the pandemic pushed her to breaking point, she encountered the life-changing love of Jesus Christ. That moment marked her complete exit from the industry, the start of deep emotional healing, and the discovery of a new identity rooted in faith instead of performance.

Today, Tessa speaks boldly about the hidden harms of the sex industry and the destructive impact of pornography addiction. Her story stands as both a warning and a beacon of hope and proof that no one is beyond the reach of freedom and redemption.

Resources and Helplines

4ps Group LLC and Trunnis Goggins II
Connect with Trunnis Goggins II and find out how you can get involved in what he is doing or if you are someone looking for help reach out to the 4ps Group and they can point you in the right direction.
https://4ps-group.com/

988 Suicide and Crisis Lifeline
At the 988 Suicide & Crisis Lifeline, we understand that life's challenges can sometimes be difficult. Whether you're facing mental health struggles, emotional distress, alcohol or drug use concerns, or just need someone to talk to, our caring counselors are here for you. You are not alone.
https://988lifeline.org/

ACT United (help to end the exploitation and trafficking of children and teens)
Their mission is to unite communities in prevention and ignite youth leadership in the movement to end online exploitation and trafficking of children and teens.
https://www.actunited.org/

Minnesota Adult & Teen Challenge
www.mntc.org

New Leaf New Life

Provides resources for overcoming addiction and re-entering society after incarceration.

https://newleafnewlife.org/

812-355-6842

The Sheila Smith Foundation

Mission: To redefine recovery, inspire hope, end stigma, and empower those in or seeking recovery from substance use, mental health issues, trauma, and related life challenges to increase their recovery capital, heal, and help others to do the same.

http://thesheilasmithfoundation.org/